Sir John Banham

Governor of the Charterhouse
July 2007 - November 2017

with deep appreciation for your enduring support

Michael Graydon

Revealing the Charterhouse

THE MAKING OF A LONDON LANDMARK

Revealing the Charterhouse

Edited by Cathy Ross
with photographs by Lawrence Watson

the Charterhouse
in association with D Giles Limited, London

First published in 2016 by GILES
An imprint of D Giles Limited
4 Crescent Stables, 139 Upper Richmond Road,
London SW15 2TN, UK
www.gilesltd.com

A catalogue record for this book is available from
the British Library

Hardcover ISBN: 978-1-907804-98-4
Softcover ISBN: 978-0-9927109-1-0

For the Charterhouse:
Curator and Editor: Cathy Ross
Production Editor: Tom Hobson
Book Designer: Joe Ewart

For D Giles Limited:
Editorial Manager: Magda Nakassis
Copy-editor and Proof-reader: David Rose
Produced by GILES, an imprint of D Giles Limited,
London
Printed and bound in China

Thanks and acknowledgements

The idea for this book originated with Dominic
Tickell: it would not exist without him. Thanks are
principally due to all the book's contributors, all of
whom worked on the book at challengingly short
notice. The Charterhouse would also like to thank
the institutions and individuals who have allowed
their images to be reproduced. Particular thanks
are due to those members of staff and Brothers
who agreed to be photographed.

Thanks are also due to: (for the Charterhouse)
Tom Hobson, who managed the supply of images,
Emma Morris, who helped with the photography
and curatorial matters, and Alan Tyrell for his
hospitality; (for D Giles Limited) Magda Nakassis,
Sarah McLaughlin, Louise Ramsay and Dan Giles.

This publication marks the completion of the
'Revealing the Charterhouse' project, which has been
generously funded by the Heritage Lottery Fund and
several other charitable trusts.

The Charterhouse wishes to thank Sharon Ament
and Finbarr Whooley of the Museum of London for
their support of the 'Revealing' project, which is a
collaboration between the Charterhouse and the
Museum of London.

Photographic acknowledgements

The Charterhouse is grateful to all copyright-
holders who have given permission to reproduce
their images in this volume. Copyright and
photographers' credits are included in the captions.
Where illustrations are uncredited, rights rest with
the Charterhouse.

The Charterhouse has made every effort to gain
permissions for the use of the images in this book.
Any omissions will be rectified in future editions.

Front cover:

Master's Court.

Photograph by Lawrence Watson

Back cover:

Charterhouse gardens.

Photograph by Claire Davies

Previous pages:

Fig 1: **Entrance Court.**

Fig 2: **Roadway from Entrance Court.**

Photographs by Lawrence Watson

CONTENTS

FOREWORD

'Revealing the Charterhouse' is a transformational project for our charity. The core purpose of Sutton's Hospital in Charterhouse, our full name, is to fulfil the charitable wishes of our founder, Thomas Sutton, as we have done since 1611. These wishes, reinforced by the Charity Commission in 2009, comprise two purposes: the care of the resident Brothers and bursary support to talented, but less well-off pupils at Charterhouse School. What is not included in these aims is the upkeep of our Grade I listed buildings.

Over the last few years it has become increasingly clear to our Governors that the Charterhouse needed to devise new mechanisms for raising funds if our duties of care to the buildings were to be discharged. Accordingly, one strand of 'Revealing the Charterhouse' is the launch of a new fund, separate to the core Hospital endowment, whose sole purpose will be to support the heritage and history of the Charterhouse, including upkeep of the buildings.

This is a new departure for us. The Charterhouse is a private foundation. Until this project the Charity has largely relied upon Sutton's beneficence. We have been greatly encouraged by the success of the fundraising that this capital project has generated and I would like to pay tribute to the work of Dominic Tickell, Development Director of the Charterhouse, who initiated the project and has steered this work.

I would also like to thank the contributors to this magnificent book: Cathy Ross, Julian Luxford, Nigel Llewellyn, Stephen Porter, Catherine Smith, Todd Longstaffe-Gowan, Eric Parry, photographer Lawrence Watson and graphic designer Joe Ewart. The Charterhouse is deeply grateful for their eloquence and hard work in creating a publication that captures the spirit of the Charterhouse as well as recounting its history.

Charlie Hobson
Master of the Charterhouse

Fig 3: **Plaque above the entrance into Master's Court:** 1611 is the foundation date of Sutton's Hospital.

Photograph by Lawrence Watson

Introduction

Cathy Ross

'The Chronicles of Charter-house abound with curious matter'[1]

'Revealing the Charterhouse' is the title of the project that has occupied staff, Brothers and governors of the Charterhouse for the last few years. The overall aim has been to open up this historic site more fully to the general public through creating new visitor facilities, a learning centre equipped for schools-use and a new museum room. The gardens in Charterhouse Square, formerly the outer precinct of the medieval monastery and more recently a gated enclave, have been replanted to accommodate increased footfall: the gates are now left unlocked on most days, allowing any passer-by to enter and enjoy the greenery at close quarters. This volume of essays is one of several strands of work within the project, all of which came to completion in the autumn of 2016 when the Charterhouse was newly revealed.

As the name implies, the 'Revealing' project took its cue from the idea that public enjoyment of this remarkable place would be best achieved through removing impediments. In 2010 an urban design study of Farringdon described the Charterhouse site as 'perhaps the last vestige of the closed, insular institutions which once characterised much of this area'.[2] 'Revealing' means that this will no longer be the case. All the various strands have fed into a process of opening up and disclosing – throwing new light into dark corners, unearthing half-forgotten items, unlocking doors, removing layers of dirt on oil paintings and generally sprucing up the public face of this venerable complex. Besides revealing, the project has also done a fair bit of adding. There are now new spaces inside the Charterhouse dedicated to the visiting public, including a small shop. Any interested party can now visit what has hitherto been largely a private space, accessible only to those who made a special effort or who knew people 'on the inside'.

After 2016 many more people than before will encounter the charms of the Charterhouse. Most visitors should leave with an understanding of what the Charterhouse is today: a thriving almshouse housing a community of personable Brothers. It is to be hoped that many will also absorb some sense of the long and sometimes turbulent past that lies behind today's flourishing institution. The land on which the Charterhouse now sits was first used in the mid-fourteenth century, as a Black Death burial ground: then partially built over to create a Carthusian monastery, which in turn was transformed during the sixteenth century into a Tudor courtyard house with a large precinct attached. In the early seventeenth century the courtyard house and precinct were both bought by a philanthropist, Thomas Sutton, and turned into an almshouse and a school under the title of 'The Hospital of King James founded in Charterhouse within the County of Middlesex'. The original school departed in 1872, at which point the Hospital shortened its name to the form under which it was commonly known, 'Sutton's Hospital in Charterhouse' or just 'Sutton's Hospital'. Today the name of the institution is even shorter. It is just 'the Charterhouse'.

The sequence of burial ground, monastery, aristocratic house, charitable foundation is not an uncommon one in England. At one level this is a simple story of pragmatic adaptation of existing buildings, a story that can be reduced to a diagram (page 14). But the Charterhouse has a particularly complex and unusually dramatic past, thanks in no small part to the site's location on the edge of the City of London. Royal attention and power politics have influenced events here: famous names flit in and out of the story. Although the site has indeed been occupied by closed insular institutions, it is also a patch of land in inner London and thus subject to all the processes that have driven change in any such

Previous pages:

Fig 4: **Two Brothers crossing Wash-house Court.**
Photograph by Lawrence Watson

Fig 5: **Thomas Sutton's coat of arms above a doorway in Master's Court.**
Photograph by Lawrence Watson

1348–1371 | BLACK DEATH CEMETERY

1371–1533 | CARTHUSIAN MONASTERY

1533–1545 | TENEMENTS

1545–1611 | TUDOR MANSION

1611–1872 | SUTTON'S HOSPITAL | SCHOOL AND ALMSHOUSE

1872–2016 | SUTTON'S HOSPITAL | ALMSHOUSE ONLY

urban plot, from road and rail building to fluctuating land values. The new museum room in the Charterhouse aims to provide a digestible outline of this eventful past, aimed primarily at visitors who need only a basic outline to help them make sense of their visit. But what about the more detailed history, the more precise understanding of what processes and events drove change? Is there a need for more revealing here?

It is something of a convention for books about the Charterhouse to begin by posing the question whether there is a need for another book on the subject, given that so many have already been written. Thus, David Knowles in 1949: 'with such excellent works already in print, there might seem to be little excuse for adding to its bulk'.[3] Fifty years later, the preface to Philip Temple's invaluable monograph for the Survey of London mused: 'It had to be asked whether there was enough to add to existing knowledge to justify such a study in the first place. Much has been written over the centuries about the Charterhouse and its buildings.'[4] This is all undoubtedly true. The place clearly has an enormous power to fascinate and there is a wealth of existing literature, much of it written by those who knew the place from the inside and fell under its spell. As Gerald Davies explained in his *Charterhouse in London* (1921), the fascination began early: 'I was for nine years a Foundation Scholar in London during which time I developed a love for the place and a zeal … for its traditions and antiquities.'[5] Davies went on to become an Assistant Master at Charterhouse School and in 1908 was appointed Master of the Charterhouse itself.

Even for those whose memories of the institution were less fond – the monk Maurice Chauncy, for example, whose purpose in writing was to set down the injustices that had occurred – the place was charged with special qualities. Chauncy falls into the category of a Charterhouse chronicler, a writer more interested in recording events and people. The other big category of Charterhouse scholars comprises the building historians, those who wrestle with the puzzle of the standing structures. 'Revealing' is really the wrong term for these architecturally minded authors. Most have been less concerned with taking away misunderstandings as adding new pieces to a maddeningly incomplete jigsaw: how did the little cloister relate to the priory church; did the Tudor bowling alley occupy the space that is now chapel cloister; where exactly was the monks' flesh-kitchen?

The customary reply to the question of whether a new book is needed is yes: new things need to be said because missing pieces of the jigsaw have been found. For David Knowles in 1949, the new discoveries were archaeological, enabling him and his co-author W. F. Grimes to pinpoint more precisely the location of the monastic buildings. For Philip Temple, work on inventories and other untapped documentary sources added new information about the Tudor mansion where hitherto 'many things were still unresolved'. For Gerald Davies in 1922 the new discoveries were simply explained by his good fortune in living in the twentieth century: 'Having survived into a day when the unearthing of much entirely fresh material has enabled us to explain much which before was inexplicable, and to set right a great many errors into which the earlier writers, for lack of this material, inevitably fell.'[6]

All in all, what might be called Charterhouse Studies starts the twenty-first century in very good shape. Philip Temple's Survey of London volume is one of four recent 'key texts' underpinning the modern understanding of the Charterhouse.[7] The second is Stephen Porter's history of Sutton's Hospital published in 2009, a definitive account of the charity drawing on the Hospital's extensive archive deposited at London Metropolitan Archives. The third is Anthony Quick's 1990 history of Charterhouse School, which has much to say about the 'Slaughter House School, near Smithfield', as former pupil William Makepeace Thackeray unkindly called it, before the school moved to Godalming in 1872. The fourth text is the 2002 monograph by Bruno Barber and Chris Thomas of Museum of London Archaeology, which not only publishes the findings

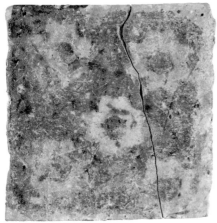

of the important 1998 excavations in Preacher's Court, but also provides an overview of all archaeological activity on the site since W. F. Grimes's investigations in the aftermath of the Second World War.

This brings us on to the present volume: is there a need for another book about the Charterhouse? There is no doubt at all that the essays that follow contain a wealth of original research and recent insights from experts in their field. All of this will add to existing understanding. But the hope is that the volume will also reflect the fascination of the Charterhouse in other ways. The distinguished contributors bring different perspectives to the subject, and all were given a loose brief precisely so that these different perspectives could be brought together in one volume. If there is an overall aim it is to show that the Charterhouse is very far from fully revealed – that the more that is written about it, the more it tantalises: its details invite scrutiny, its links to the wider world promise new clues. In this sense the book is less a synthesis of existing knowledge and more a 'taster', designed to tempt future scholars, writers, artists and photographers to take an interest. Much remains to be explored: there is no full-length biography of Thomas Sutton; the part played by the many women who lived and worked in the precinct – Anita Armstrong, for example (Fig. 12), one of the few women with a memorial plaque inside the Chapel – remains a hidden history.

The written essays start with Julian Luxford's compelling account of the lived experience of the Carthusian monk. The story of the monastery also establishes the point that the Charterhouse cannot be fully understood without the context of ideas and beliefs from which its institutions sprang, in this case the extraordinary disciplines of Carthusian monasticism. His account is also a reminder that, despite appearing today to embody serenity and continuity, the Charterhouse's past has been interrupted by violent change. This point is reinforced by Stephen Porter's account of the Tudor courtyard house. The seventy years between the suppression of the monastery in 1538 and

the acquisition of Howard House by Thomas Sutton in 1611 are dizzy with disruption: abrupt changes of ownership as fortunes rose and fell; demolition and construction in abundance; the long shadow cast by the shocking deaths of the monks.

Stephen Porter is the Honorary Archivist of the Charterhouse and no one knows the buildings or the documentary history of Sutton's foundation more intimately. His chapter on Sutton's Hospital traces the evolution of the institution from Sutton's original idea to the way his wishes are realised today. This chapter falls between two contributions focusing on particular aspects or episodes within the Sutton's Hospital era. The first, by Nigel Llewellyn, provides a detailed analysis of Sutton's monument in the Chapel together with some background about the life of Sutton himself. Catherine Smith draws on the archive of Charterhouse School to explore the lived experience of the nineteenth-century schoolboys who knew the place well.

The final essays are from the two architects responsible for the physical changes associated with the 'Revealing' project. Eric Parry discusses the idiosyncratic buildings in the light of his other architectural projects at Canterbury Cathedral and elsewhere. Todd Longstaffe-Gowan, the landscape architect responsible for replanting the Square, traces the history of the outer precinct of the monastery, contrasting its 'ancient impenetrability' with the aims of the current redesign, preserving the Square's special qualities of seclusion whilst at the same time opening it up. An expert in historic squares, he draws attention to the Charterhouse's ecological importance as a place for bird and plant life, as well as for people. No less important than the texts is the photographic essay by Lawrence Watson that runs throughout the book. The brief was to capture the rhythm of the Charterhouse day, but not necessarily as a strictly documentary exercise. His atmospheric pictures represent an evocative creative response to the particular qualities of this remarkable place.

Figs 6, 7: **Medieval floor tiles, excavated from the site of the great cloister, 1990.**

© Museum of London

Fig 8: **Medieval metal mount, probably from a book, excavated from Preacher's Court, 1998.**

© Museum of London

A SENSE OF PLACE

'It is not too much to say that by the terms of Sutton's original foundation, the inhabitants of London were made the co-beneficiaries of his charity'[8]

'Revealing' has underlined the Charterhouse's dual identity as a place of public heritage and private charity. The first duty of the governors is to pursue the aims of the registered charity, as derived from the original objects of Thomas Sutton's charity of 1611, confirmed by Act of Parliament in 1628:

- the relief of beneficiaries (Brothers) by the provision of accommodation and care or in such other ways as the Governors think fit; and
- the advancement of education by the provision of financial support to the School (i.e. Charterhouse School)

Yet the governors are also guardians of 'heritage assets' of considerable importance: not just a complex of Grade I listed buildings but also collections of historic items, including paintings, decorative art, rare books, photographs and social history items, alongside the institutional archives of the hospital and the school. The public interest in preserving these heritage assets for future generations to enjoy is considerable, a fact acknowledged by the Heritage Lottery Fund, which has supported the 'Revealing' project financially.

The new focus on heritage stewardship is reflected in new wording for the Charterhouse. Until recently Sutton's Hospital focused on the fact that it was 'founded 1611'. The recently adopted strapline for the Charterhouse is 'living the nation's history since 1348'. In other words, the institution now thinks of itself as a place; its sense of identity now stretches back to events three centuries before the institution was born. This could, of course, be said to be an example of an institution moving very slowly and eventually catching up with the common understanding. From the nineteenth century onwards most writers on Sutton's Hospital have reinforced the belief that the charitable foundation somehow evolved from the genes laid down in the fourteenth century by the Carthusian priory. And most have agreed that the history embedded in the Charterhouse site is more than just institutional and local. As 'a Carthusian' wrote in 1847, 'The era of the Reformation is unquestionably the most interesting and important in our history, whether considered with reference to religion or to our civil polity; and the Chronicles of the Carthusian order throw a clear and vivid light on many passages in that eventful period.'[9] This change of wording for the Charterhouse is slight but nevertheless marks an official shift in emphasis that establishes a new outlook for the future.

The fit between the Charterhouse as an independent charity and as a heritage guardian has not always been so harmonious. In the mid-1880s battle was joined between the governors of Sutton's Hospital and building preservationists, led by the Society for the Protection of Ancient Buildings under the fiery leadership of William Morris. At issue was not just the fate of the historic buildings but the more revolutionary question of who had the moral rights to decide – the property-owners

Fig 9: **One of several nineteenth-century names scratched onto the glass window panes in the great chamber.**

Photograph by Lawrence Watson

Stereoscopic Co.

54. CHEAPSIDE E.C.

or those who spoke for the public interest. In 1885 the governors prepared a scheme, set out in a Parliamentary Bill, proposing that the Brothers be moved from the site and treated as 'out-pensioners', the nineteenth-century equivalent of care in the community. The idea was that each elderly man would be found a place to live and be supported by a regular annuity of £100 from the charity paid directly to their families, landlords or carers. The new scheme, it was argued, would enable more Brothers to be provided for.

The sting in the tail was that by moving the Brothers out, the governors would then be left free to develop the Clerkenwell estate, their plans for which involved demolishing some almshouse buildings. Although the governors protested that the Tudor building, Howard House, was excluded from their plans and therefore under no threat, the scheme met with ferocious opposition. The preservation of London's more ancient buildings was something of the *cause du jour*. The Charterhouse had already attracted the attention of the Society for Photographing Old Relics of London, which had recorded its buildings in 1880; the newly formed Society for the Protection of Ancient Buildings took up the case with zeal. In December 1885 letters to *The Times* led to a leading article and further thundering that 'to mutilate any part of buildings which are one of the few links with the past, and which are consecrated by literary and historical associations' was 'an act of vandalism'.[10] *The Times* went on to bemoan the 'bold, bad ways of modern developers intent on rooting out anything which is ancient'.

The Times adopted quite a bold position itself, arguing that Thomas Sutton's gift to London of an almshouse and school could be assumed to be a gift to the collective London public and not just the Brothers and scholars who benefited directly from the charity. The governors should take this into account: 'the inhabitants of London – their interests – we would almost say their rights – must not be overlooked'. This argument was largely about preserving the Charterhouse's open ground in an increasingly built-up area: 'the policy of depriving the people of London of a large open space in their midst, for the sake of securing these more or less questionable advantages … is quite indefensible'. Thomas Sutton, speculated *The Times*, would have thoroughly disapproved of the land in the Charterhouse precinct being sold off for productive use: 'it is at least a legitimate inference from his actions that he intended to stamp his London property with the impress of unproductiveness'.

In response, the governors offered to trade the loss of any historic buildings for the gain of a public garden, offering to develop the former Brothers' burial ground on the northern edge of the site as an ornamental park 'permanently dedicated to the public and accessible to all'.[11] The loss of historic buildings was rather dismissed, by one of the governors, as negligible: 'London abounds in the antique and can easily spare these not very attractive portions of this estate.'[12] The preservationists disagreed and in the event the Bill was withdrawn, to the slight disappointment of William Morris who was spoiling for a further fight. Like *The Times's* leader writer, Morris saw the historic Charterhouse buildings as the property of the public, not the governors. He told the annual meeting of the Society for the Protection of Ancient Buildings in June 1886:

> We have, however, scored one great success – I mean, in connection with the Charterhouse. It does seem to me, and to most of us, that the original scheme of the people who wanted to destroy it was one of the most audacious attempts at robbery of the public that has ever been attempted, and that it ought to have been treated harder than it was. I am only sorry that the Bill was withdrawn, and was not rejected.[13]

The fight over the fate of the buildings in the mid-1880s was fuelled by the particular circumstances of that decade. London's older charities were coming under intense and often hostile scrutiny as

Figs 10, 11: **Photographs of Master's Court (above) and Preacher's Court, c.1890.**

Fig 12: **Anita Armstrong, Matron of the Charterhouse, 1904–1922.**

Carte de visite by the London Stereoscopic Company, c.1910.

questions were asked about their actual contribution to the public good. At the same time, alarm at the vulnerability of ancient buildings was swelling to a crescendo as a new wave of warehouse construction, roads and railways threatened to leave London without any surviving timber-framed buildings. The border between Clerkenwell and the City was a particular place of concern with the rebuilt and modernised Smithfield Market bringing new levels of noise, traffic and industrial activities into the area. At the bottom of Charterhouse Square, the building of the Metropolitan Railway in the 1860s and the construction of a new access road to Smithfield in the 1870s had already swept away any remains of the gentry houses that had once stood there.

We live in rather different times today. But, nevertheless, the events of the 1880s have resonances with the 'Revealing' project in 2016. The broader public interest in the site has to be weighed against the duties of the charity. Today's governors should be congratulated for achieving what promises to be a good balance with benefits for both public and Brothers. In the twenty-first century public benefits are not just about increased physical access; engagement and participation are important ends. The new learning centre will enable thousands of schoolchildren every year to engage with medieval monks and Tudor nobles in richly evocative surroundings. A new volunteer workforce will be recruited to help the Charterhouse catalogue, manage and research its collections: in time this work will create digital access to the heritage collections through the website, enabling thousands of items to be better known and better used.

The future benefit to the Brothers is also about engagement, participation and sharing a heritage in which they already take pride. The project was designed to preserve the privacy of the Brothers: the residential parts of the site remain private and no visitor is allowed to wander at will. The project also proceeded on the understanding that Brothers individually or collectively chose how much or how little they engaged with it at any particular stage. From the beginning, some of the Brothers were enthusiastic contributors to the various strands of work, and this looks set to continue as the nature of the work changes from planning to delivery. For those Brothers who choose to engage, the most important contribution is leading public tours round the buildings, a role that Brothers already take on, and which visitors value highly: feedback indicates that 'meeting a Brother' is as much a highlight of a tour around the Charterhouse as seeing the historic interiors.

In the project's early days the Brothers were asked to choose some words that they felt best described their life at the Charterhouse. At a lively meeting the following emerged:

> Community, Independence, Security, Mutuality, Tranquil, Historic, Current Benevolence, Contribution, Experience, Home, Tolerance, Co-operation, Diversity, Sharing, Cornucopia, Balance, Stimulating, Humour, Jovial, Caring, Unique, Special.

At the same time, there was much discussion about the need for 'Revealing' to achieve its aims without imperilling 'the Charterhouse DNA', hesitatingly defined as:

- Authenticity – this is a real place: the building has been a witness to history;
- Intimacy – this is a place where you get under the skin of London's past;
- Home – this is a place where people live, and still do.

These are words from today, but the human warmth they express is surely in part an accumulation from the past, a legacy firmly embedded in the character of the London Charterhouse.

Fig 13: *A Rainy Day*, watercolour by Harold Hookway Cowles (1896–1987), a Brother in the last years of his life.

References

1 'A Carthusian' [W.J.D.R.], *Chronicles of Charter-house* (London, 1847), 1.

2 East with Alan Baxter & Associates, *Farringdon Urban Design Study, Part 1: Baseline Study*, London Borough of Islington, March 2010, p. 15; available at www.islington gov.uk/publicrecords/library/Environmental-protection Quality-and-performance/Reporting/2011-2012 (2012-03-03)-Part-1-Historty-and-heritage.pdf (accessed 11 March 2016).

3 David Knowles and W. F. Grimes, *Charterhouse: The Medieval Foundation in the Light of Recent Discoveries* (London, 1954), xi.

4 Baroness Andrews, Preface to *The Charterhouse*, ed. Philip Temple, Survey of London Monograph 18 (New Haven, CT, 2010), v.

5 Gerald S. Davies, *Charterhouse in London: Monastery, Mansion , Hospital, School* (London, 1921), vii.

6 Ibid., viii.

7 The four key texts referred to in this paragraph are: Philip Temple, *The Charterhouse*, Survey of London Monograph 18 (New Haven, CT, 2010); Stephen Porter, *The London Charterhouse* (Stroud, 2009); Anthony Quick, *Charterhouse: A History of the School* (London, 1990); Bruno Barber and Christopher Thomas, *The London Charterhouse*, Museum of London Archaeology Service Monograph 10 (London, 2002).

8 *The Times*, 29 December 1885.

9 'A Carthusian', *Chronicles of Charter-house*, 1.

10 The leader was published in *The Times*, 29 December 1885. The quotation is from a subsequent article, 8 May 1886.

11 Letter from the Archbishop of York, *The Times*, 29 December 1885.

12 Letter from A. Styleman Herring, Parish Priest of St Paul's, Goswell Road, *The Times*, 2 June 1886.

13 William Morris, 'Speech Seconding a Resolution to Establish a Fund for the Repair of Ancient Buildings', 9 June 1886, *Annual Report of the Society for the Protection of Ancient Buildings* (London, 1886), 65–9; available at www marxists.org (accessed 11 March 2016).

Fig 14: **Doodles by William Makepeace Thackeray, drawn when a pupil at Charterhouse School, 1822–8: part of the Waley-Cohen collection of Thackeray material held at the Charterhouse.**

Photographer Lawrence Watson was commissioned to record a day in the life of the Charterhouse in February 2016. Fewer than a hundred people actually live in the precinct and a further hundred or so arrive every day to work. Not every activity is captured in these images, but they evoke the daily rhythm of life and particular visual qualities of the Charterhouse. Lawrence commented,

> 'I am drawn to odd viewpoints and slanting light, and there's a lot of both here. It's a fascinating place to photograph – full of patterns you don't really see at first, then they emerge when you look again – the light seems to come from nowhere.'

a day in the life of the Charterhouse

1: early morning

5.30	Kitchen staff arrive.
7.00	The night porter opens the gates into Charterhouse Square and the entrance doors into the Charterhouse itself.
7.15	The Charterhouse flag is raised. The flag shows the arms of Sutton's Hospital; it is replaced with the Union Jack on appropriate days.
7.55	The bell rings for chapel service.
8.20	Breakfast cooked and served for the Brothers.

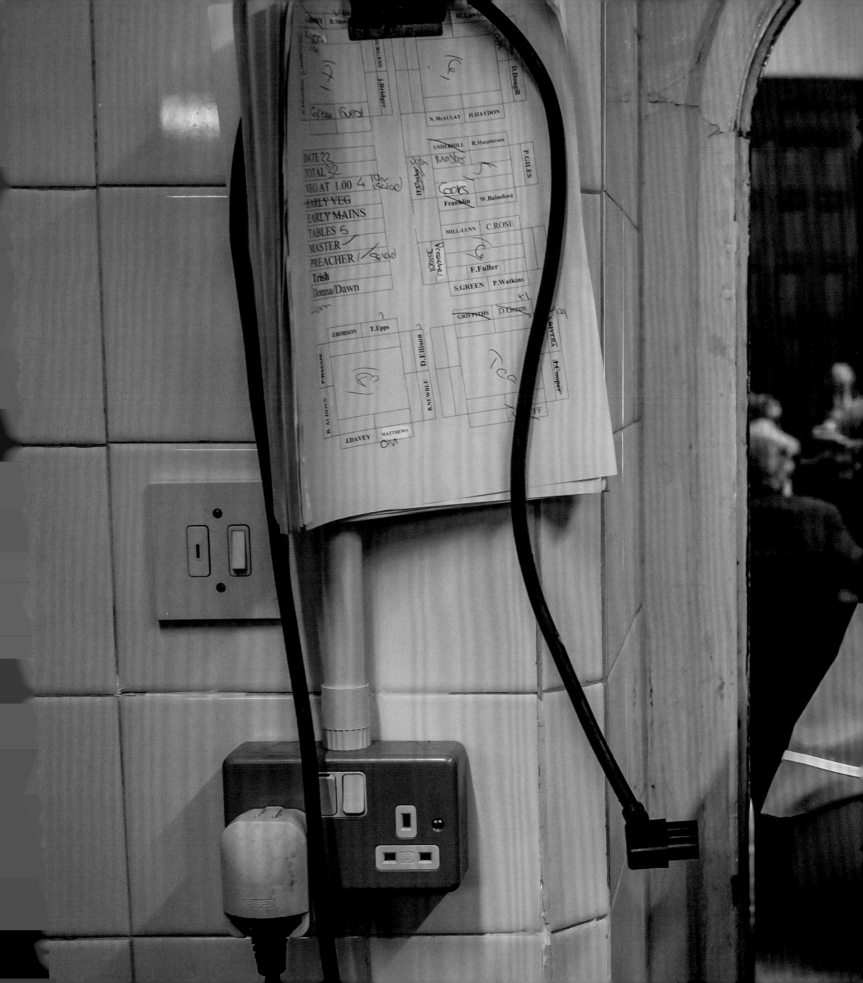

At þe begynnyng of þe charturhous god dyd schewe
to þe bysschop of Gracionapolitane þaynt Hewe
Seuen sterres goyng in bryhtnes to þat place
Wher now þe ordur of þe charturhous abydyng has
And when moo syttes at þat place had bene

Carthusian Monasticism and the London Charterhouse

Julian Luxford

THE CARTHUSIAN ORDER

From its foundation in 1371 to its dissolution in 1538, the London Charterhouse owed much of its reputation to a powerful contradiction it embodied. It was simultaneously a miniature wilderness, populated by world-denying hermit-monks, and an integral religious and economic part of a teeming metropolis. One cannot understand this ambiguous status, or the monastery in general, without some knowledge of the religious order to which the Charterhouse belonged. 'Beneath every history, another history', as the novelist says.[1] Accordingly, this chapter begins with a synopsis of that order, paying special attention to its moving spirits, customs and development in England.

In the later eleventh and the twelfth centuries, monasticism in Western Europe experienced a change of climate. Before this time, the Benedictines and their reformed offshoot the Cluniacs had stood in more or less splendid isolation. Between the 1070s and 1120s, however, a number of other orders were established in what amounted to a monastic reform movement.[2] Overwhelmingly, the seeds of this activity were sown in France and Italy, but most of the new orders quickly spread to other countries. None of these orders emerged overnight. The process of building and endowing their mother-houses, recruiting brethren and obtaining papal and political recognition for them usually took several years and sometimes several decades. However, specific years of foundation are always assigned because they seem authoritative and provide an anchor to which subsequent history can be attached. In the case of the Carthusian order, 1084 is recognised as the foundational year. This was when Bruno (c.1030–1101), a cleric from Cologne who had lived for many years in France, retired to the mountains above Grenoble with six companions eager to lead an eremitic life under his guidance. Within a short time these men had settled on the site of what became the Grande Chartreuse, the mother-house of the Carthusian order. The order's name is taken from the alpine massif that towers over this monastery and is called in Latin *Cartusia*, whence the French *Chartreuse* and the English *Charterhouse*.[3]

In 1090 Bruno was summoned away by Pope Urban II and soon founded a second charterhouse in Calabria. The dissemination of Carthusian monasticism thus began almost immediately. During the twelfth century the order grew steadily but modestly, mostly in the mountains of southeast France: by 1200 there were thirty-seven charterhouses. However, as the Carthusians came to the attention of those willing and able to set up monasteries, the numbers increased more quickly. A wave of foundations occurred in the later Middle Ages, and by 1550 some 225 charterhouses had been founded. Of these, twelve were for Carthusian nuns, but most were male-only establishments containing a mixture of choir monks and lay brethren.[4] A class of inmate called the *clericus redditus* also existed (this Latin term is a technical one and thus not readily translated). Like ordinary monks, these *redditi* dwelt in individual cells and could, under certain conditions, take their place in choir, but were not usually subject to the full rigours of monastic life. This peculiar status suited the scholars and secular officials who sought admission to the order in increasing numbers in the 15th century. A well-known English *redditus* is John Blackman (d. 1485), a chaplain and biographer of King Henry VI, who was an inmate of the London Charterhouse in the late 1450s.[5]

Unlike St Benedict, Bruno wrote no Rule to serve as a blueprint for monastic life. Around 1127, however, the fifth Prior of the Grande Chartreuse, a man named Guiges du Pin (or more simply Guigo), wrote down a series of customs informed by Bruno's attitudes and

Fig 15: **Page from an English Carthusian manuscript of the fifteenth century, with drawings of episodes from the foundation history of the Carthusian order.**

London, British Library, Add. MS 37049, fol. 22.
Reproduced by permission of the British Library Board

practices.[6] This customary is usually referred to as the Carthusian Rule. As time went by, it was augmented by legislation issued by the Grande Chartreuse. Collections of statutes, compiled to help monks maintain their spiritual integrity under increasingly trying circumstances, were published by the order in 1259, 1368 and 1509/10.[7] But Guigo's customs always remained the bedrock of monastic conduct and still give the clearest idea of what it meant to be a medieval Carthusian. Presented in eighty short chapters, their main themes are the performance of religious ritual, acts of monastic charity, the monk's way of life, the officials of the charterhouse (cook, baker, tailor and so on), the necessities of existence (including food, drink, clothing and shaving) and the treatment of new monks, along with those who had run away or been expelled. The language is unambiguous, for Guigo was a plain dealer who viewed monastic life in largely black-and-white terms. Choir monks were to live as contemplatives rather than manual labourers. This fundamental requirement explains the need for lay brothers, who lived in the same monasteries but apart from the choir monks, and were permitted to do agricultural and other sorts of work in the open. Guigo was adamant that choir monks should never leave the charterhouse. Utter poverty was mandatory, so that no monk might own anything or accept a personal gift. A late copy of the statutes, written in English at either London or the charterhouse of Sheen (near Richmond), states that anyone found to have owned private property after he had died was to be dug up and displayed 'as an example to the rest'.[8] Monks were not to associate with outsiders under any circumstances. Thus, all contact with their families had to cease on entry to the order. A separate chapter, seasoned with biblical precedents, is devoted to the prohibition of women from the monastery.[9] A Carthusian's main 'outreach' activity was to copy religious books, which Guigo neatly characterised as 'preaching with the hands'. Mostly, monks were to pray in silence, attend as required in church and maintain unquestioning obedience to their prior.

Attendance in church was a comparatively infrequent matter for a Carthusian. Unlike the monks of other orders, he sang only two of the eight canonical 'hours' in choir (that is, matins during the night and vespers in the evening).[10] Each morning he also attended a communal mass. On major religious feasts all offices were celebrated communally in church. Most of the time, however, the monk sang the canonical hours, other than matins and vespers, alone in the privacy of his cell. Here, too, he spent much time in prayer and worked on simple tasks that could be accomplished alone, including tending the small, enclosed garden in which Carthusian cells were usually set. His was essentially a solitary, anonymous existence, to the extent that his meals were served him through a wall-hatch and his cell marked not with his name but a single alphabetic letter, and occasionally some devout verses. (Letters and verses both existed at the London Charterhouse, and the letters are referred to again below.)[11] The only communal meals were taken at noon on Sundays and major feast days, when monks sat without speaking and listened to readings from scripture or some commentary on the Bible. Their general condition of hermit-like solitude and the distinctive, intense kind of spirituality that accompanied it is celebrated in the last chapter of Guigo's statutes, and has always remained fundamental to Carthusian life.

Anonymity was symbolised for the Carthusian by his clothing. His habit, of white wool, comprised a long-sleeved gown, belted at the waist, with the distinctive mantle called a scapular worn over it. The scapular had a high-peaked cowl that made the face hard to see, and baggy, horizontal strips of cloth that hung down at the sides below the waist. These strips immediately distinguish Carthusians from members of other religious orders with white habits, such as the Cistercians and Premonstratensians. The Carthusian's shoes were of cow's leather and he also had woollen mittens, should he need them. His diet was extremely simple. Where St Benedict counselled a general moderation

and forbade his monks only the flesh of quadrupeds, Guigo was much more rigid: 'On Monday, Wednesday and Friday we will content ourselves with bread and water, and whosoever wishes may also have salt'. Vegetables and a modicum of wine were served in addition to this on Tuesday, Thursday and Saturday, while on Thursday some cheese was allowed, if there was any to be had. At the communal meals on Sunday there was salad, and cheese, fish or eggs were permitted if available. From mid-September until Easter the monks had only one meal a day, except on the solemn religious feasts observed by the order. For the rest of the year, two meals were served on Tuesdays, Thursdays and Saturdays. As with St Benedict, whose Rule Guigo knew, it is a measure of monastic priorities that the subject of food is not addressed until chapter 33 of the customary. It is hard to escape the idea that the Carthusian considered eating to be a sort of necessary evil, and that food, as a requirement of man's 'animal nature', had the potential to corrupt his spiritual life. This attitude was supported by the sorts of texts Carthusians preferred, not least the letters of St Paul: 'Food for the belly and the belly for food; but God will destroy both one and the other' (I Corinthians 6:13).

Such austerities did nothing to inhibit the growth of the order outlined above. Recruits were not wanting. With this growth came an inevitable increase in the number of celebrities the Carthusians produced. Few were more important than Hugh of Avalon (d. 1200), a monk of the Grande Chartreuse who ended his days in England as Bishop of Lincoln. He was soon canonised and, although French, added an insular note to Carthusian history as the first prior of an English charterhouse (at Witham in Somerset). As time went by, it became increasingly expedient for the Carthusians to promote the history of their foundation and sing the praises of their saints. Doing so advertised the order's fidelity to ascetic principles that were widely and progressively more valued in an age of developing

Fig 16: The 'Tree of Bruno' image from the *Tertia compilatio statutorum ordinis carthusiensis* (The third collection of the statutes of the Carthusian order), published at Basel in 1510.

cynicism about monastic life. Series of narrative images representing Bruno's establishment of the Grande Chartreuse were often displayed in charterhouses, and even made their way into luxurious Books of Hours made for Jean de Berry (d. 1416), the culture-loving brother of King Charles V of France (Fig. 15).[12] The order's foundation and growth were differently represented in another, more diagrammatic, image. This was published in 1510, in the first printed edition of the Carthusian statutes, a volume that certainly existed at the London Charterhouse.[13] The 'Tree of Bruno' is a sensible name for it, as it shows the founder lying on the ground with a tree growing from his heart, with branches populated by some of the saints and saint-like monks the order had produced (Fig. 16). The model for this was the so-called Tree of Jesse, a popular medieval image invented to encapsulate the royal genealogy of Christ. Guigo is represented directly above Bruno, and Hugh of Avalon has a place high up on the left. The Virgin Mary and the eremitic John the Baptist stand on either side of the tree. Carthusians were particularly devoted to these two saints. A discarded mitre and crosier symbolise Bruno's refusal of an episcopal post in favour of the monastic life. The backdrop is an unpopulated wilderness. This image summarises how late medieval Carthusians understood their order's history and principles, and how they wished these things to appear to outsiders.

THE CARTHUSIANS IN ENGLAND

For administrative purposes, Europe's charterhouses were divided up into provinces. From 1368 there was a separate English province, of which the London Charterhouse quickly became the nerve-centre due to its size and location.[14] With the foundation of the only Scottish charterhouse at Perth in 1429, this province reached its maximum extent of ten monasteries.[15] For such a wealthy country, and one so densely populated by religious houses, this small total is remarkable. It is particularly puzzling that no charterhouse was ever founded in East Anglia, and neither was there one anywhere in the rural south between Dover and the West Country. Indeed, until the mid-14th century England had only two charterhouses. These were St Hugh's monastery at Witham, which had been founded in 1178–9, and another at Hinton, also in Somerset, founded in 1227. Thereafter, the following houses were established in quick succession: Beauvale, in Nottinghamshire (1343), London (1371), Kingston-upon-Hull (1377), Coventry (1381), Axholme, in north Lincolnshire (1397–8), Mountgrace, on the North Yorkshire Moors (1398), Sheen (1414) and finally Perth. Much of the initiative and finance for these foundations came from members of the nobility. At Witham (Henry II), Coventry (Richard II), Sheen (Henry V) and Perth (James I), kings were directly involved. Most of these English charterhouses were of the normal size, with sufficient space and buildings to accommodate a prior and 12 choir monks. However, London, Sheen and Mountgrace were larger, with the largest, Sheen, designed to accommodate 30 choir monks.

The English charterhouses were relatively wealthy monasteries. When a national census of monastic income was taken in the mid-1530s, the least affluent of them, Coventry, was reckoned to have £131 per annum at its disposal. The wealthiest, Sheen, had £800; next came London, with £642. The latter two houses, with more monks and servants to support, were more costly to run. Such totals mean little nowadays to anyone except an economic historian, and it would be pointless to calculate their equivalents in current money. A better way of putting them into context is to observe that the poorest monasteries of any order in England were subsisting on less than £20 per annum, while the wealthiest, the great Benedictine abbeys of Glastonbury and Westminster, had substantially more than £3000 each.[16] Nearly all monastic income came from a combination of rents and leases on real estate and tithes from parish churches (it has been estimated that the tithe-income of about 15 per cent of English parish churches was transferred to larger religious institutions between 1300 and the Reformation). By the 14th century, when most of the English charterhouses were established, it was hard for anyone to find the resources for such endowments. As well as a short supply of real estate, royal laws existed that placed stringent conditions on the gifting of lands to religious institutions.[17] Only the seizing of revenues from 'alien' religious houses in England, which were smaller monasteries directly governed by larger ones located in France, enabled Henry V to set up Sheen. (London also benefited by this confiscation.) These circumstances, and the very close control of land by the Crown, do much to explain why relatively few charterhouses were founded in England in spite of widespread respect for religious austerity. Henry V and Cardinal Wolsey were among those to single the Carthusians out as shining examples of religion, but by the time they did so, the foundation of new monasteries was a very difficult business.

London, Hull and Coventry charterhouses all stood close to large centres of population. This reflects an important development in later medieval Carthusian practice, and one in which the founding of a charterhouse near Paris in 1257 was highly influential.[18] The Carthusian ideal, of course, was to live in deserted places where monks could apply the principles set out in their customary without any secular disturbance or temptation. The location of the Grande Chartreuse exemplifies this. A significant difficulty with maintaining it was that those able to finance charterhouses were generally reluctant to have their investments invisibly buried in rural obscurity. Rather, they required status symbols, monasteries that would be seen and thus reflect well on their piety and power. Importantly, they also wanted the very high religious standards of the Carthusians to be visible to as many people as possible. The order's founding fathers did not anticipate the paradox that the solitary

monk could most effectively convey his object lesson in a city or large town, where his asceticism would be most conspicuous. Yet this was clear enough to Michael Northburgh (d. 1361), the Bishop of London who co-founded the London Charterhouse. He wrote in a letter to the priors of Hinton and Witham that he thought God would welcome a charterhouse near the capital city, because (to quote him) 'a house so placed will the more advance in a few years the spiritual building up of many [people] than all the [charter]houses of England have advanced from the time when they were first founded'.[19] Henry V, who founded Sheen, also understood the contribution that frank manifestations of religious virtue made to political stability at a time when talk of heresy was on the rise.[20] Indeed, to understand properly the value placed on the Carthusian order in late medieval Europe, it is necessary to take into account not only the monks' reputation for principled behaviour but also the means by which this reputation spread.

THE FOUNDATION OF THE LONDON CHARTERHOUSE

In medieval documents, the London Charterhouse is routinely said to be 'by' or 'near' (*juxta*) London, rather than actually in it. This does not mean that the monastery was essentially separate from the city, but simply that it stood outside the medieval walls. The story of how and why the site in West Smithfield was chosen has often been told, first of all by the Carthusians themselves in a short chronicle contained in their surviving register.[21] It is part of a pre-history of the monastery that illustrates well the protraction and prevarication that often surrounded the foundation of individual monasteries, but which was generally glossed over later in order to suggest unwavering resolution on the part of founders. The principal actor was a knight named Walter Manny (his name derived from the lordship of Masny in Hainault), who settled in England in 1327 and fought with King Edward

III in Scotland, the Netherlands and France. As a soldier and diplomat, Manny was a complex character, loyal, generous, gallant and horribly brutal by turns. As he grew older, the latter aspect of his conduct must have generated a good deal of metaphysical heart-searching, for he believed unquestioningly in purgatory and divine judgement. He thus had a strong motive to champion religious causes. In 1348 he leased a thirteen-acre plot of land called Spitalcroft (the 'Hospital's croft') from the hospital of St Bartholomew in Smithfield, and allowed it to be used as a cemetery for victims of the Black Death. This was consecrated for use in January 1349 in honour of the Holy Trinity and the Salutation of the Virgin Mary. The latter dedication, which commemorates the Annunciation of Christ's incarnation (Luke 1:26–38), was subsequently adopted for the Charterhouse. Early claims that Spitalcroft received up to 100,000 dead are greatly exaggerated, but certainly hundreds and perhaps some thousands of people were buried there. The recent excavation of some of their skeletons has given a keen sense of the peculiar, evocative nature of the Charterhouse's site. Manny had a chapel built on the Spitalcroft, which he planned to enlarge into a college of thirteen secular priests. This would in fact have been a more normal course of action for someone of his social position than the foundation of a charterhouse. His largesse was part of a distinctive charitable trend. The Bishop of London, Ralph Stratford (d. 1354), had established a plague cemetery immediately to the north in the previous year, and Edward III founded a Cistercian abbey, St Mary Graces, on another such cemetery in East Smithfield in 1350. [22]

Manny received papal permission to found his college, but the project never advanced: he was probably reluctant to commit the money needed for it at a time when he was still relatively young (he was born around 1310) and expensively active in the king's service. At some point after his consecration as bishop in 1354, Michael Northburgh approached Manny about founding a charterhouse on the Spitalcroft, or New Church Haw (the 'New Churchyard') as it had become known. He offered to act as co-founder and put his money down, providing 1000 marks (£666) towards the enterprise immediately and leaving a further £2000 in his will. The chronicle of events contained in the late medieval register of the Charterhouse attributes Northburgh's zeal to a visit to the charterhouse near Paris, and the ensuing reflection that there was no Carthusian monastery in his own diocese. This is no doubt accurate. The fact that visiting a charterhouse could have a transformative effect on a subtle, earnest mind is seen elsewhere in the later Middle Ages in such celebrated intellectuals as Petrarch, Jean Gerson, Marsilio Ficino, Pico della Mirandola and Thomas More. [23] Manny agreed to the proposal and an agreement to the effect was sealed in May 1361, shortly before Northburgh's death. Northburgh then wrote to the priors of Hinton and Witham, urging them to collaborate. He pointed out that there were already urban charterhouses near Paris, Avignon, Bruges, Saint-Omer, within the city of Cologne and elsewhere. The priors seem to have responded with interest, but both of them, and Northburgh himself, died before further progress was made.

Had Northburgh not died when he did, then the foundation date of the London Charterhouse would almost certainly be 1362 or 1363. By his agreements with Manny, the bishop assumed full responsibility for further progress, and his energy in pursuit of the matter was prodigious. The resuscitation of the scheme thereafter evidently had more to do with the Carthusians themselves than with Manny. While the circumstances are not fully known, it seems likely that another Prior of Hinton, a man named John Luscote, followed up Northburgh's suggestion after consulting with the Grande Chartreuse. He made an appointment with Manny to discuss the situation and was encouraged to further action. As Northburgh had adopted the project, Manny must have felt that it was up to the bishop's executors, and the Carthusian order, to further it. Moreover, he probably lacked the time and expertise to do the work personally, setting up a charterhouse being a specialised business. Manny was, however, not diffident about the project's success, if only for the sake of his own spiritual health. Hence, he remained committed to it throughout the 1360s, when various obstacles to progress were put in Luscote's way. Some of these obstacles evidently arose because nearby religious institutions were reluctant to accept another into their midst. At the time, this part of north London was home to various populations of monks, nuns, regular and secular canons, Knights Hospitallers, secular priests and recluses. The medieval chronicle in the Charterhouse's register names the dean and chapter of St Paul's Cathedral and the master of St Bartholomew's hospital among the opponents. These people, acutely sensitive to the temper of their environment, must have realised that a house of Carthusian monks would attract a great deal of patronage that might otherwise come their way.

A significant practical problem seems to have been that Manny needed to own the Spitalcroft rather than simply leasing it if he was to found a permanent monastery there. Whatever the hospital's objections, he managed to secure the site in 1370. In the same year, at his personal petition, the Grande Chartreuse agreed that Luscote could leave Hinton for London to oversee the construction of temporary buildings and recruit the first monks. A *clericus redditus* named John Gryseley joined him from Witham, and the chapel already planted in the cemetery served as their place of worship. Luscote quickly recruited six other monks, two each from Witham, Hinton and Beauvale. One of these, named Benedict, was a lay brother. His recruitment at the outset is telling of the compromised situation of the new community. As noted, a lay brother could fetch and carry in a way forbidden to choir monks. Luscote in particular must have felt acutely exposed. His role necessarily involved him in much travel, negotiation and commerce. For example, almost as soon as he came up from Hinton, he was obliged to go to Chelmsford in Essex to petition

for the Bishop of London's help in a conflict with St Bartholomew's hospital. All of this activity, however justifiable in pursuit of a religious goal, must have caused him both anxiety and compunction in light of the Carthusian commitment to a silent, cloistered anonymity. Luscote and his brethren were surely relieved when Manny secured the official foundation charter on 28 March 1371. This did not conclude Luscote's worldly business. His activities continued, largely unabated, until his death in 1398. However, it afforded the legitimacy needed to tap the generosity of London citizens, whose support would, in time, pay for most of the Charterhouse's buildings and underwrite the monks' rarefied way of life.

The official foundation of the Charterhouse also allowed the Grande Chartreuse to appoint Luscote as prior. Hitherto, his title had been the practical but undesirable one of 'rector'. In the course of its history, the London Charterhouse was to have 13 priors, but none, including the martyr John Houghton, exceeded Luscote's commitment to his office, and all were deeply indebted to him for advancing so far the spiritually compromising business of setting up their monastery. Although we know little about Luscote, it is clear that he was an articulate and persuasive negotiator, and he had the backing of a sacred cause. These things helped him a good deal with the really urgent requirements of his work in the 1370s. These requirements were fundamentally interlinked. In order to accommodate the monks suitably, he had to arrange construction of permanent buildings, at least partially made of stone. But for that purpose, sufficient land was needed to build on. The original thirteen-acre site was not large enough for the envisaged double monastery of twenty-five choir monks. Then, of course, stone buildings were expensive (this is discussed below), so the fledgling monastery needed gifts: of money, cash-generating privileges such as parish church revenues, and property that could be rented out to provide permanent streams of income.

BENEFACTIONS AND BUILDING

In theory, the business of getting the monastery off the ground should have been jump-started by Michael Northburgh's bequest of £2000. But it is unclear how much of this money ever reached the monks, and some historians think little or none of it did.[24] While he lived, Manny was able to help by acquiring parcels of land to augment Spitalcroft, and his reputation also influenced the generosity of other people. Manny died in January 1372, but the terms of his will and ostentatious burial in the choir of the monastery's church meant that his intentions were remembered by those obligated to him. Thus, in 1376, King Edward III transferred to the Charterhouse some property that Manny had owned but not bequeathed to the monks. The hospital of St Bartholomew also made additional grants, one of which was necessary for the completion of the cloister and monastic cells. By 1377 an adequate site had been cobbled together. Further grants of land made later by the Knights Hospitallers (in 1384) and monks of Westminster Abbey (in 1391) gave the Carthusians space for a large orchard, a communal vegetable garden, a hayfield and an uncultivated, miniature 'wilderness' inhabited by rabbits and other small game. The central complex of buildings thus had relatively generous grounds to both north and south, and in all, the monastery occupied about 30 acres.[25] The open space gave the monks somewhere to conduct the vigorous walks that Carthusian communities took together after the noon meal on Sundays in order to relieve the physical and psychological pressure of confinement. (On these walks, monks were allowed to discuss religious topics.) If one thinks of the London Charterhouse as a prison for its monks (and this was, and still is, a common Carthusian metaphor for the monastery) then the outer precinct functioned as an exercise yard.

By his will, Manny assigned the Charterhouse £4000 owed him by Edward III and the Black Prince, along with two apparently valuable properties, the manor of Knebworth in Hertfordshire and a half-share of the manor of Ockholt in Kent. (The monks recorded that they paid for the other half of Ockholt using Northburgh's money.) While Luscote the monk was a professional idealist, the realist in him can hardly have dared to hope for the £4000. If so, then this was prudent, for the king and his son, who were both dead themselves by the middle of 1377 and always cash-strapped while they lived, never paid it. But it must have been a harsh blow to his ambitions when Ockholt, in Romney Marsh, was flooded with the loss of its buildings and animals, and had to be sold at a knockdown price. Knebworth, too, was lost in the law courts, and this was also the fate of other lands and revenues pledged by early benefactors or purchased outright by the monks themselves. Looking back over a century or so, the writer of the chronicle could rationalise these losses as evidence of the fortitude of Luscote and his companions, and also of God's commitment to the ultimate success of the monastery. In material terms, however, it is clear that the monks realised little benefit by Manny's will. The founder must, at least, have paid for his own tomb, a richly painted and gilded object with carved heraldry and (though no trace of it survives) an alabaster effigy. Two pieces of the tomb-chest have been recovered and are now displayed in the Charterhouse, along with the leaden bulla of Pope Clement VI found in his grave.[28] These fragments testify to high-quality workmanship and a design incorporating a continuous arcade of miniature vaulted niches that has much in common with the stone bases of medieval saints' shrines (Figs 17, 18, 19). Although nobody ever considered Manny a saint, the monks thought extremely highly of him and extolled his piety. In their eyes, the pompous tomb was a concession to his labours in their service.[29]

In spite of the failure of Manny's bequests and early losses to litigation, the location of the Charterhouse effectively assured its future. For one thing, it came to the notice of most of the powerful churchmen who travelled to London on business. Bishops of Lincoln and Durham were among its early benefactors. Further, Luscote was able to attract the patronage of influential London citizens, whose example inspired the generosity of others in turn. This gift-giving eventually became a sort of fashion in its own right, and so widely diffused that it is common to find small amounts left to the Charterhouse in the wills of people who lived far away and had probably never seen it. Thus, for example, John Ode (d. 1496), vicar of Thornham in Norfolk, left the monks 26s 8d, and it would be possible to cite many similar bequests. [30] Small sums like this might have been applied to any purpose, but much of the substantial lay patronage went towards building. This indispensable activity was a constant drain on resources, and in fact there was no point at which the Charterhouse was definitively 'finished' in a structural sense. The architecture of medieval monasteries tended to evolve and mutate over time rather than simply starting and stopping. However, it was also something to which people of means wanted to contribute, for buildings, as large, useful, material things, helped their patrons' names to be remembered in the long term. Providing them was thus part of a strategy for attracting the prayers that medieval people thought they needed for a prosperous life and quick passage through purgatory after death. Nobody could afford (or anyway wished) to build the Charterhouse outright, so the work went ahead piecemeal. This process, and the ongoing nature of Luscote's efforts to solicit contributions, is suggested by the fact that the monastery was still not functionally complete three decades after its foundation. Among the essential buildings lacking at the turn of the fifteenth century were six of the monks' cells, a chapter-house where the community could assemble to discuss administrative matters, a refectory, an infirmary and a parlour where the prior could receive important guests. The cloister, church, precinctual wall and aqueduct system were also unfinished. These works, which the monks estimated would cost upwards of £1730, were completed later, as benefactors came forward. [31]

This estimate was presumably much less than what had already been spent during Luscote's time as prior. Keenly aware of the debt entailed by patronage, the monks wrote memoranda about those who paid for their cells and built the chapels annexed to their church. Copies of these survive in the register. As first founder of the monastery, Manny was credited with building the cell marked A, although it is known that he did not pay for all of it. Sir William Walworth (d. 1385), a lord mayor of London, funded cells B, D, G, H and J, partially out of the estate of another lord mayor, Sir John Lovekyn (d. 1368). [32] Adam Fraunceys (d. 1375), a merchant, paid for cells C, E, F, L and M. In this case, we have a sum to reckon with, for the memorandum states that Fraunceys gave 1000 marks sterling (£666) towards this work. This puts the cost of a cell at roughly 200 marks (£133), an estimate loosely reflected by other bequests. Thomas Hatfield, Bishop of Durham (d. 1381), gave 600 marks for cells R and S. One Thomas Aubrey and his wife Felice gave 260 marks to found cell N. Margaret Tilney, a prosperous laywoman, contributed the same sum for cell O. Later on, probably in the 1430s, William Symmes (d. 1439), a wealthy grocer, gave 1040 marks, which paid for cell Y and also other works, including much of the aqueduct system by which water was brought into and expelled from the cloister. The completion of this system was commemorated by a remarkable drawing, made in the mid-15th century and still kept at the Charterhouse. Here, the plan of the claustral complex could at last be shown complete (Figs 20, 21). Although the size of the conduit-house is greatly exaggerated in this drawing, its central location in the cloister nicely illustrates the symbolic as well as practical value of water to the whole monastery, something William Symmes was probably aware of. [33]

Slow progress and high cost were consequences of architectural ambition. While it would have been possible to build much more extensively in wood, as was done at other charterhouses (Coventry, for example), the London monastery was planned with stone buildings of superior quality from the outset. The surviving parts of the gatehouse,

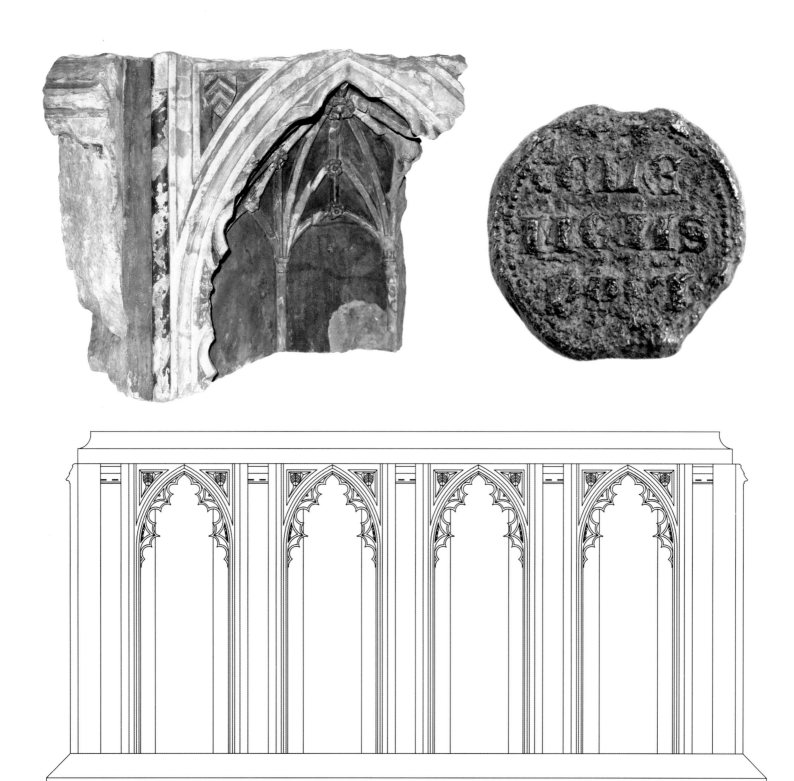

church, cells and other buildings reflect this (Fig. 22). If a Carthusian church was a relatively cheap affair due to its small size, the cloister, with its cells like two-storey houses, was correspondingly expensive. The founders' aspirations are clear from the fact that Manny and Luscote contracted Henry Yevele (d. 1400) to design the first cell and the cloister. Yevele was the most celebrated architect of his day, and simply to obtain his services was a prestigious achievement. Among his other projects were the naves of Westminster Abbey and Canterbury Cathedral, various works at the Tower of London and the remodelling of Westminster Hall for King Richard II. To sympathise with the expense involved, one has to appreciate the figurative and imaginative force of elegant stone buildings for late medieval people. In a monastic setting, such buildings advertised the dignity of the monks and their religion. Their cost was also considered an oblation to God, and they were a fitting evocation of the monastery's symbolic status as a microcosm of heaven. It would have struck medieval Londoners as both eccentric and distasteful if the monks had chosen to save money and live in a walled-off hovel.

The fittings within the monastic church, and no doubt in some of the cells, were also of a quality that surpassed strict need. Guigo's statutes gave little guidance on the subject of church ornaments. They simply forbade anything of gold or silver except the chalice and reed that came into contact with the blood of Christ at the Eucharist.[34] However, the Grande Chartreuse later translated the spirit of this minimalism into detailed legislation, and there is proof that London's monks were aware of the fact. In a fifteenth-century volume of Carthusian statutes in Latin compiled at the Charterhouse, it is stated that representations of women and the coats of arms of laymen are banned because they contradict the simplicity and humility of the Carthusian order, whether they appear in stained glass windows or elsewhere. A warning is also sounded against embellishing altars with tables of 'curious' (that is, ingeniously made) imagery.[35] Simplicity of ornament was the official

watchword. The statute is dated 1424, and as such legislation was almost invariably reactive, it reflects the fact that many charterhouses already contained such things by this date. London certainly had its share. While we know nothing of stained glass, Manny's tomb in the choir was set with heraldry, and an inventory of the church's contents taken in 1539 reveals much about tables of imagery on altars.[36] The high altar was dignified by a retable carved from 'bowne' (presumably ivory) and 'made with small images curiously'. These represented the Passion of Christ, perhaps in a series of individual scenes. Matching this was a frontal of alabaster, showing the Holy Trinity and 'other images'.[37] Alabaster was the material of choice for small-scale religious carvings in late medieval England, and its whiteness suited it nicely to Carthusian use. The altars in the subsidiary chapels were also attractively set forth. There was another retable of alabaster, depicting Christ's Resurrection, in St John the Evangelist's chapel. An altar set against the screen dividing the choir from the nave was dignified by an image of the Virgin Mary's Assumption into heaven. A large figure of Christ crucified rose above this screen, and smaller crucifixions with Mary and John stood in the two chapels jointly dedicated to saints Jerome/Bernard and John the Baptist/Michael. In St Catherine's chapel there was another retable with the Holy Trinity on it, flanked by the four 'doctors' of the Latin Church (SS Ambrose, Augustine, Gregory, Jerome), while in another chapel on the north side of the choir, two retables with St Anne on them are listed. In this instance, the fact that there was a chapel dedicated to St Agnes in the same location suggests that one of these may in fact have represented that saint. There were also images of the Crucifixion at two altars in the chapel of the Holy Cross at the west end of the church, and an alabaster retable showing the Seven Joys of the Virgin at an altar in the chapter-house, which abutted the church to the north-east.

Many other images standing on or near the altars are also specified in this inventory. The document says nothing of images not associated

---

Fig 17: **The larger of two surviving fragments of Walter Manny's tomb.**

Fig 18: **Leaden** *bulla* **issued by Pope Clement VI, found in Walter Manny's tomb. It was originally attached to a licence to choose a deathbed confessor, issued to Manny in 1351.**

Fig 19: **Conjectural elevation of the chest of Walter Manny's tomb, based on the surviving fragments.**

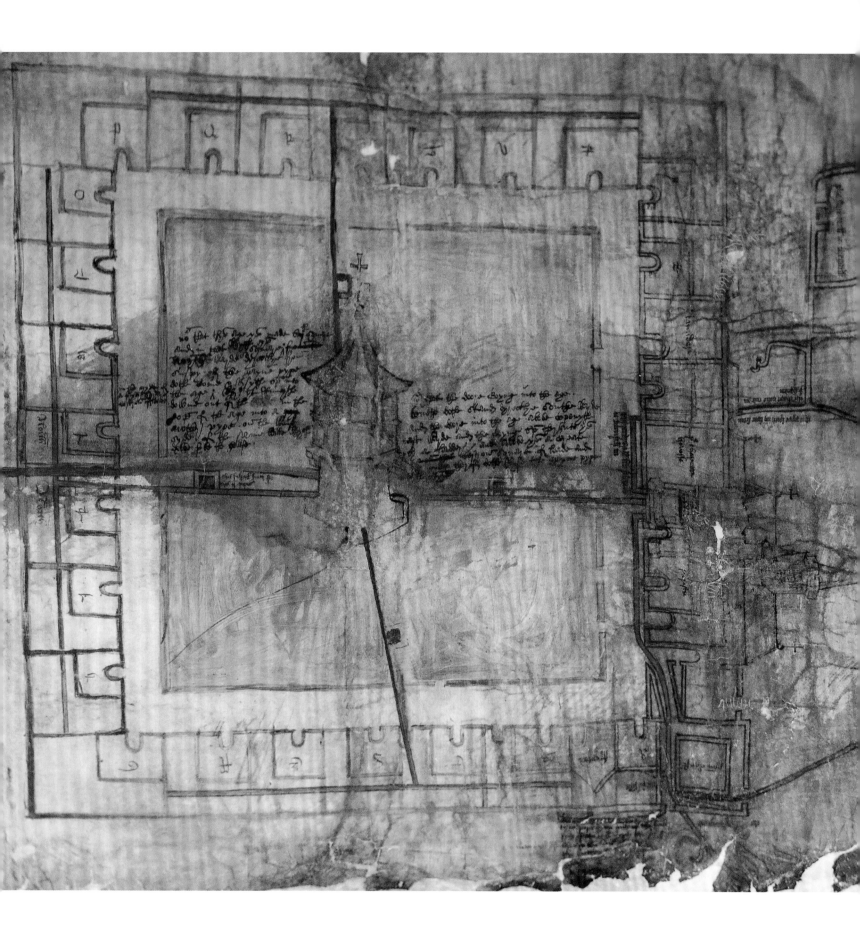

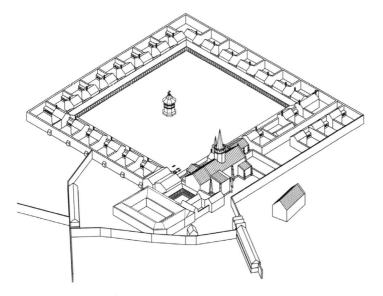

with altars, but probably there were such in the windows and painted on the walls. As the event commemorated by the monastery's dedication, the Salutation of the Virgin by Gabriel must have been depicted somewhere. There is no mention of a beautiful sculpture of St Catherine of Alexandria, which survives in part thanks to its redeployment by Reformation-era builders (Fig. 23). This is the only significant piece of medieval figure-sculpture to remain from the London Charterhouse. It represented the saint standing on the Roman emperor Maxentius (her persecutor) and holding a large book in fingers of the elongated, tapering sort that Van Dyck would later give his aristocratic female sitters. The trademark spiked wheel and sword are missing along with the right arm, as is the crowned head with its high brow and flowing hair. Presumably, this sculpture also occupied the chapel of St Catherine, which stood on the north side of the nave and was paid for by Sir Robert Rede in 1518.[38] Catherine was an appropriate choice for Rede, who as a Cambridge man and senior magistrate had reason to identify with the patron saint of scholars. She was certainly suitable to Carthusian monks, who associated Catherine with eremitic monasticism (her body was thought to have been carried by angels to the desert monastery on Mt Sinai). The book she holds is also nicely symbolic of Carthusian interests in religious literature and their commitment, mentioned above, to 'preaching with the hands'. The connection of Catherine with erudition is further shown by the images of the doctors of the Latin Church, each a prolific, inspired author, at the altar of her chapel.

This sculpture, and the other images mentioned here, may seem difficult to reconcile with the pious statute of 1424. However, the prohibition against representing women obviously cannot have been meant to disqualify images of female saints, while the 'curious' character of the high altarpiece and evident sophistication of the other retables and fittings was doubtless acceptable to the monks on the grounds that it did honour to God and orthodox religion. It was, anyway, hard

Fig 20: The 'waterworks drawing' showing the plan of the Charterhouse's central complex around the middle of the fifteenth century.

Fig 21: Three-dimensional reconstruction of the central complex of the London Charterhouse as it stood around 1532.

From B. Barber and C. Thomas, *The London Charterhouse* (2002), fig. 56: reproduced by permission

Fig 22: The main inner gatehouse of the London Charterhouse. The lower storey dates from the fifteenth century, and is typical of such buildings in pairing a wide entrance arch for vehicles with a small one for pedestrians.

to refuse devout gifts, which many of these items presumably were. As early as 1382, a London alderman, Sir Robert Launde, bequeathed £20 for a retable for the high altar 'by the best painter' in the city.[39] This may or may not have been identical with the 'bowne' object recorded in that location in 1539. Launde wanted his own image, or his name at least, included on his gift, a request that neatly represents the unavoidable permeation of an urban charterhouse by outsiders. For good measure, he also asked to be buried in front of the choir stall from which the prior sang matins. Burial of laymen in charterhouses was another privilege interdicted by Guigo and later extended only to founders like Manny. But it went ahead anyway, both at London and elsewhere, for medieval people found the idea of burial inside a monastery extremely comforting and went to great lengths to obtain it. By the dissolution, the London Charterhouse probably contained more than 100 non-monastic graves, many embellished with handsome monuments. All that such breaches of policy reflect is the difficulty of satisfying both a very strict idealism and the reality of monastic dependence on secular generosity, which always came at a price. It would be wrong to think that the monks were happy with the situation, however well they were able to rationalise it. It would also be misguided to see rule-breaking of this sort as symptomatic of spiritual laxity. All of the evidence suggests that London's monks maintained rigorous observance to the end, and the fact that the altars where they said mass were decked with elaborate images had no practical effect on that rigour.

CONSOLIDATION AND DISSOLUTION

These thoughts about patronage and the art and architecture of the London Charterhouse have taken us beyond the period of foundation and into that of institutional consolidation.

Only a flavour of the monastery's history in the century before its dissolution can be given here. The Charterhouse is relatively well documented, and thanks to this there are various positions from which to consider its everyday life. Religious activity, encompassing ritual performance and less regulated devotion, is perhaps the most obvious one. A matter of interest here is the large number of chantry foundations based in the monks' church. A chantry was a round of daily commemoration established, often in perpetuity, by a wealthy person for the health of his or her soul after death, along with the souls of friends and family members. It involved hiring a priest able to say mass every day for this purpose and securing the use of an altar where he could do so. Evidently not all of the chantry priests attached to the London Charterhouse were Carthusian monks. Some were non-monastic, secular priests who came into the monastery to do their work but did not live there. Sir Robert Rede, for example, wanted a secular priest to serve his chantry in St Catherine's chapel. Other commemorative obligations involved the monks personally. In 1505 they agreed to celebrate the anniversary of the death of King Henry VII's queen, Elizabeth of York (d. 1503), 'yearly for ever while the world will endure'. After the king died, his soul was also to be prayed for. A focus for the commemoration was set up next to Manny's tomb in the choir in the form of a hearse covered with cloth and decked with four candles at the cardinal points, each weighing seven pounds. According to this agreement, 'every monk then being in the said house of Our Lady a priest and present at the said anniversary shall in every day of every such anniversary say mass of requiem'. There is a proviso, exempting monks who were ill or 'bound to say other masses in the said house of Our Lady on the same day'.[40] This reflects the fact that some of the choir monks (all of whom were priests) had to celebrate on behalf of the souls of other benefactors and their families. As priests were only supposed to say mass once a day, those who had this obligation had to be excused participation in the royal anniversary masses, although they may still have contributed to other prayers said on the occasion.

Economic life is another interesting aspect of the Charterhouse's later history. As suggested, no monastery could survive without close and continuous management of the properties and privileges that generated its revenue, and the need to buy in goods and services was steady, particularly for use in winter and spring. Large numbers of original documents testifying to this activity survive in the monastery's register and in other collections now held at the National Archives in Kew. There is a particularly rich seam of material from 1492 to 1500, in the form of the accounts of the monastery's procurator.[41] The procurator was a Carthusian administrator (a choir monk, not a lay brother or *clericus redditus*) whose job was to manage those mundane affairs not within the remit of the prior or lay brothers. He was constantly involved in getting and spending, overseeing real estate and negotiating acquisitions of new property. The accounts in question relate to two successive procurators, John Cootes and Phillip Underwood. They provide a detailed breakdown of the annual income yielded by the Charterhouse's holdings. For instance, in 1492 the rent on land and tenements in Charterhouse Lane realised some £12 17s 8d, properties on Aldersgate Street generated £10 10s and others at the Barbican and Redcross Street £7 5s 4d. Properties in Bishopsgate Street, Fenchurch Street, Cornhill, Grace Church Street, St Lawrence Lane, Candlewick Street, Watlingstreet and elsewhere brought in similar sums. It appears that even the gardens within the Charterhouse's walls were rented out, to the tune of £13 9s 8d. Among the tenants were doctors, servants of the monastery, merchants and artisans. Some of them were foreigners, one being designated 'frenchman' and another 'hispanico'.[42] A vivid impression arises from all this of the importance of rent income to the monks, the localness of its sources and the fragmentary nature of the Charterhouse's property portfolio. This complexity indicates in turn the piecemeal character of late medieval benefaction, the small size of properties available to the monks for purchase and the challenges of the procurator's job.

The development of material and intellectual culture at the Charterhouse is also an important matter for which evidence is available. Intellectual work was naturally dominated by religion, but not to the exclusion of other subjects. The manuscript of the statutes written in English mentioned earlier in this chapter contains the stricture that 'nobody of our order, either on his own or another's behalf, in the monastery or elsewhere, may dare to practise the arts of alchemy or making quintessence'.[43] Of course, there would have been no point to this if Carthusians were not widely dabbling in alchemy already, as monks and canons of other orders often did in the late Middle Ages. A particularly interesting aspect of intellectual activity involves the making, use and distribution of books. As well as the register, some twenty-five manuscript books survive from the Charterhouse, along with a handful of early printed ones. Lists of books now lost also survive, and these show that London's monks lent copies of various works to other English charterhouses. The existing volumes reside in libraries as far afield as Yale University, although the majority is in Cambridge, London and Oxford.[44] Almost all are written in Latin, which was the choir monks' normal language. Those in English contain texts of interest to the Carthusians that were not available in Latin. They may have been useful to the lay brothers, who were not always Latinate. Without exception, the texts are religious. Within this class, there are several categories: constitutional books dealing with the order's rules and regulations; liturgical books used in rituals; books of private devotion; commentaries of various sorts and speculative texts, some of them authored by mystics (including the famous *Cloud of Unknowing*). None is more physically impressive than a large fifteenth-century Bible in English now in the Bodleian Library at Oxford. This has numerous pages with illuminated borders, and a unique woodcut engraving of King Henry VI as a saint pasted into the back (Fig. 24).[45] Passages in this manuscript are marked up for reading in Easter week and 'in the

refectory'. The choir monks certainly did not need to be read to in English, but the lay brothers presumably did, so the directions probably relate to them. There is also an early inscription stating that the Bible had actually belonged to Henry VI, and was later given to the London Charterhouse. The inference is that it was a royal gift, which would have made it particularly valuable to the monks.[46]

The British Library holds a small manuscript profoundly suggestive of the tenor of Carthusian devotion around the year 1500. It is not generally acknowledged to have come from the London Charterhouse, but Ian Doyle, the great scholar of English Carthusian books, has argued convincingly that its scribe was a London monk named John Wetham.[47] The manuscript contains a popular contemplative text called the *Rosary of the Blessed Virgin Mary*, a calendar listing the dates of fixed religious feasts throughout the year (including those of Bruno and Hugh of Lincoln) and four woodcut images, pasted in as meditative aids for use either independently or in conjunction with the text. There are also pages painted black and spotted with drips of red, and others painted red with slightly darker red drops on them. This is an extremely unusual, perhaps unique, feature. The idea was to evoke the suffering of Christ. The red pages in particular suggest Christ's raw skin, oozing blood from the many wounds inflicted by flagellation and other tortures. On one such page, a woodcut representing a Carthusian monk kneeling at the feet of the resurrected Christ is set in the middle of the gory field (Fig. 25). This image itself is liberally sprinkled with red drops. There are speech-scrolls in Latin, by which the Carthusian beseeches Christ to direct him towards salvation and is told to flee the world, conquer his urges, remain silent and be at peace. Underneath, there is a consolatory verse in English, stating that 'The greatest comfort in all temptation / Is the remembrance of Christ's Passion.'

This expression of what is sometimes called 'blood piety' is largely out of step with modern tastes. However, if we turn away from

Fig 24: **Unique woodcut image of King Henry VI as a saint, pasted into a Bible from the London Charterhouse.**

Oxford, Bodleian Library, MS Bodley 277, fol. 376v. Reproduced by permission of the Bodleian Library

The greatest comfort in al temptacyon.
Is the remēbraunce of crystes passyon.

it then we miss an opportunity to appreciate the most urgent concerns of practically any Carthusian. The whole point of the monk's solitude was to help him develop the personal relationship with God that he considered necessary for the salvation of his soul. This relationship involved suppression of the ego and utter subjection to the divine will. It was a very challenging thing to cultivate. An effective way of doing so was to dwell on the human aspects of divinity, because these touched on the essential condition of the monk himself. The human worshipper could relate to the human Christ more directly than to the ineffable Holy Trinity. In particular, Christ's suffering offered a focus for meditation, because, of course, the monk was implicated in it. Like all Christians, he believed Christ's death a necessary condition of his own salvation. The implication involved feelings of guilt as well as expectation and joy, not least because sins were thought to hurt Christ as long as they were committed. As this page suggests, pious reflection on the messy, painful nature of Christ's bodily death functioned to intensify the monk's experience, partially by heightening his emotional vulnerability and partially by manifesting the idea that the holy blood cleanses the soul. To sprinkle the monk in the woodcut with blood was to express a hope that his soul would be made spotless through unquestioning devotion.

With hindsight, this outpouring of blood looks prophetic, for the dissolution of the London Charterhouse, 167 years after its foundation, involved a deliberate killing of monks not seen in England since the days of the Vikings. While the subject is unpalatable to anyone sympathetic to monasticism, or for that matter interested in medieval buildings, it adds a certain lustre to the Charterhouse and its order, which were loved for their adherence to principles and remained steadfast even unto death. In 1534 commissioners acting for King Henry VIII obliged religious institutions in England to take something called the Oath of Succession.[48] This entailed recognition that Catherine of Aragon

had not been Henry's lawful wife, that his recent marriage to Anne Boleyn was legitimate and that Anne's offspring by Henry would rightfully succeed to the throne. While almost everybody took this oath, London's Carthusians refused. Their spokesman was their prior, John Houghton, originally a member of the Essex gentry and scholar of law at Cambridge. Houghton had entered the monastery in 1515 and lived as austerely as any from that time. His principles were those of his monks, but as the community's figurehead he was taken to the Tower of London for his refusal, along with the procurator, Humphrey Middlemore. Pressured in this way, they agreed to sign the oath, and the other monks subsequently signed it as well, although some held out until intimidated by armed men. But the monastery remained in crisis, for it was widely and accurately predicted that further, more stringent royal demands would follow.

By successive Acts of Parliament from November 1534, Henry required all his subjects to recognise him as supreme head of the Church in England in place of the pope. Refusal to do so constituted an act of high treason, a capital crime punished with appalling cruelty. London's Carthusians had no intention of acknowledging Henry in favour of the Vicar of Christ, although they understood the consequences. Houghton was arrested again, along with the priors of Axholme and Beauvale charterhouses (the latter of whom, Robert Laurence, was a London monk by profession). He was imprisoned and examined in the presence of the king's vicar-general, Thomas Cromwell. All three men were subsequently tried and executed at Tyburn on 4 May 1535 (Fig. 26). On 19 June, three more London monks shared their fate, including Humphrey Middlemore. In prison, these men were shackled, foot and neck; on the scaffold, they were hung by the neck until half-dead, cut down, disembowelled while conscious and then beheaded and cut up, the parts of their corpses being displayed in public places *pour encourager les autres*. One of Houghton's arms was exhibited on

Fig 25: **Page from a devotional manuscript probably made at the London Charterhouse. The spattered red paint is meant to suggest drops of the holy blood.**

London, British Library, MS Egerton 1821, fol. 9v.
Reproduced by permission of the British Library Board

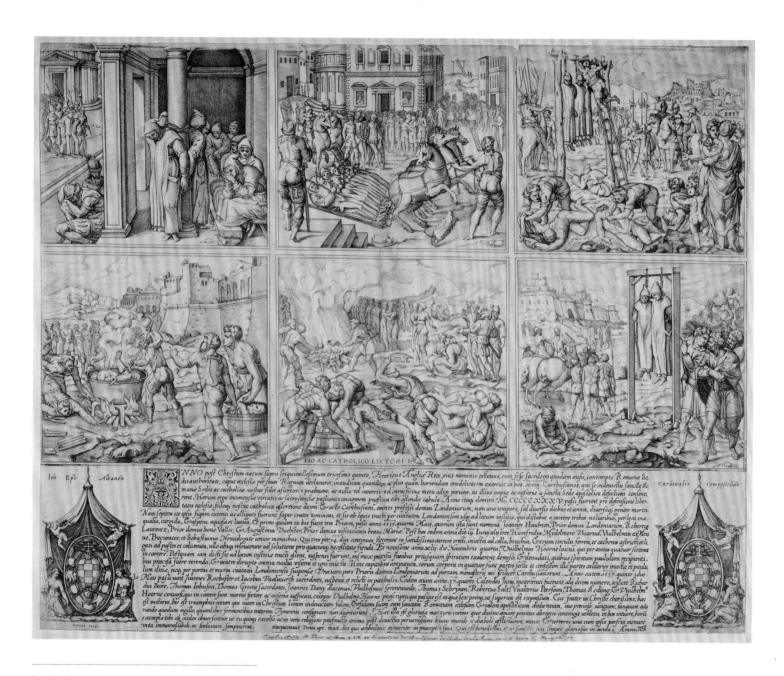

Fig 26: Six scenes of the persecution of the
Carthusian Martyrs. This engraving, published in
Rome in 1555, is luridly idealized, but can hardly
exaggerate the horrors the Carthusians endured.

Guildhall Library p5369098

the Charterhouse's gate, a grotesque parody of the medieval practice of displaying coats of arms in such locations. Cromwell, who had to strike a nice balance between deterring obstinacy and getting his master the reputation of tyrant, constantly harassed the remaining monks. In an attempt to weaken their corporate resolve, twelve were banished to other charterhouses, and monks from elsewhere were introduced at London. Finally, the Charterhouse was threatened with closure. Today, realising that all English and Welsh monasteries were soon to be dissolved in any case (not one was left after 1540), the modern observer may miss the dreadfulness of this threat, but the monks lacked the benefit of hindsight. Under such an awful cloud, many of them did formally acknowledge the king's supremacy over the Church. The document they signed and sealed survives, a tedious, humiliating piece of legalese rendered poignant by the presence of twenty individual signatures. The following excerpts sufficiently convey its substance.

> We the prior and convent of the house of the Salutation of Our Lady of the Carthusian order near London swear that henceforth we shall utterly renounce, refuse, relinquish and forsake the bishop of Rome and his authority, power and jurisdiction … and that from henceforth we shall accept, repute and take the king's majesty to be the only supreme head on earth of the Church of England … Given in our chapter-house under our common seal the 18th day of May in the 29th year of the reign of our said sovereign lord king Henry VIII. [49]

The seal of green wax appended to this document shows the Archangel Gabriel saluting the Virgin Mary ('Hail Mary, full of grace, the Lord is with thee!'; Fig. 27). As the quotation above suggests, its presence was required as a mark of the Charterhouse's submission. However, because its imagery reflects the dedication acknowledged by the pope in the 1370s, it may also have consoled the frightened and weary monks.

This was not the final end. Ten monks who had refused to sign were imprisoned and left to starve or die of illness. The only survivor, one William Horne, a lay brother, was eventually butchered at Tyburn as Houghton had been. By the time this happened, in the summer of 1540, the Charterhouse had been officially dissolved. On 15 November 1538 it was put into the hands of royal administrators, who pensioned off its seventeen choir monks. Six lay brothers were turned out with nothing, for the Crown evidently did not regard them as monks proper. Yet six other lay brethren had died in the persecutions, along with a total of eleven choir monks who had professed at London. [50]

Inventories of Charterhouse property were soon made, and the site and buildings rented and then sold off. A decade after John Houghton's death, the monastery's conversion into one of the city's fanciest private houses was underway. The irony of this is only underscored by the survival of Houghton's initials in the brickwork of the west side of Wash-house Court. [51] The early modern history of the Charterhouse is taken up in the next chapter of this book. Its progress inevitably led to radical alterations, because the fabric of a charterhouse was fit for only one purpose. However, the hidden survival within the reconstituted buildings of medieval fragments like those from Manny's tomb and the St Catherine sculpture, lodged there like elements of a genetic code, is a salutary reminder of the place's origins and fundamental character.

◆

'Nul bien sauns payn'. This French maxim is written in sixteenth-century handwriting at the end of the volume of Carthusian statutes in Latin compiled at London, mentioned earlier. [52] 'No good comes without effort' captures the spirit of it. In all likelihood, this was written after the dissolution of the monastery, and perhaps after the book had been removed from site. But it seems, nevertheless, to be a reflection on the statutes themselves, whose terse commands on subjects from abstinence to praying for the dead epitomise the earthly privations that Carthusian monks were prepared to endure for the sake of eternal bliss. As such, it can be set alongside the official Carthusian motto, 'The cross stands steady as the world turns' (*Stat crux dum volvitur orbis*), as a less abstract, more existential summation of belief. If it has a special significance at London in light of the documented sufferings of the 1530s, it also serves to remind us of a lived experience that was constant, anonymous and ultimately unknowable to all save the monks themselves.

Fig 27: **Impression of the common seal of the London Charterhouse, showing the Archangel Gabriel addressing the Virgin Mary.**

Kew, The National Archives, document E25/82/2.
Reproduced by permission of The National Archives

References

1 Hilary Mantel, *Wolf Hall* (London, 2009), 66.

2 An accessible account of this period is found in C. H. Lawrence, *Medieval Monasticism: Forms of Religious Life in Western Europe in the Middle Ages* (London, 1984, rev. Abingdon, 4/2015).

3 C. M. Boutrais, *The Monastery of the Grande Chartreuse* (London, 1893), is a classic, readable account of this monastery.

4 A. Gruys, *Cartusiana: un instrument heuristique*, 2 vols and supplement (Paris, 1976–8), gives the only clear overview of numbers, foundation dates and locations of houses.

5 R. Lovatt, 'The Library of John Blacman and Contemporary Carthusian Spirituality', *Journal of Ecclesiastical History*, XLIII/2 (1992), 195–230.

6 The standard modern edition is Guigues Ier le Chartreux, *Coutumes de Chartreuse*, ed. and trans. M. Laporte (Paris, 1984, rev. 2001), which gives the statutes in Latin and French. There is no English language edition.

7 Printed by Johannes Amerbach as *Tertia compilatio statutorum ordinis carthusiensis* [The third collection of the statutes of the Carthusian order] (Basel, 1510).

8 London, British Library, MS Add. 11303, fol. 8or–v.

9 On this interesting subject see J. Hogg, 'The Carthusians and the Temptations of Eve', in *Spiritualität Heute und Gestern*, 15, Analecta Cartusiana 35.15 (Salzburg, 1992), 138–86.

10 The canonical hours are matins (also called nocturns or vigils), lauds, prime, terce, sext, none, vespers and compline.

11 M. Hennessy and M. G. Sargent, 'The Verses over the Cell Doors of London Charterhouse', in *Studies in Carthusian Monasticism in the Late Middle Ages*, ed. J. Luxford, Medieval Church Studies 14 (Turnhout, 2008), 179–97.

12 The Belles Heures, now in the Cloisters Museum, New York (fols 94–7) and the Très Riches Heures, now in the Musée Condé, Chantilly (MS 65, fol. 86v). See J. Luxford, 'Texts and Images of Carthusian Foundation', in *Self-Representation of Medieval Religious Communities: the British Isles in Context*, ed. A. Müller and K. Stöber (Münster, 2009), 275–305.

13 See n. 7. A copy from London may survive in Gonville and Caius College at Cambridge, bound together with a hand-written collection of statutes and decrees (after 1526; MS 732/771).

14 The fullest study of the English Carthusians remains E. M. Thompson, *The Carthusian Order in England* (London, 1930). More recent and accessible is G. Coppack and M. Aston, *Christ's Poor Men: the Carthusians in England* (Stroud, 2002).

15 For political reasons, Perth was not always part of the English province. The only Irish charterhouse, at Kinalehin in Galway, existed for just forty-two years and was dissolved in 1321, before an English Carthusian province existed.

16 On Carthusian and other monastic income, see D. Knowles and R. N. Hadcock, *Medieval Religious Houses: England and Wales* (London, 1953, rev. 1971).

17 That is, the mortmain ('dead hand') legislation, first introduced by King Edward I in 1279 and subsequently augmented.

18 *La Chartreuse de Paris* (exh. cat., ed. I. Charles et al.; Musée Carnavalet, Paris; 1987).

19 The letter, written in Latin, survives in the Charterhouse's medieval register (see n. 21). This quotation comes from W. H. St John Hope, *The History of the London Charterhouse from its Foundation until the Suppression of the Monastery* (London, 1925), 11.

20 J. Catto, 'Religious Change under Henry V', in *Henry V: the Practice of Kingship*, ed. G. L. Harriss (Oxford, 1985), 97–115.

21 Made c.1500 and now at The National Archives at Kew (document number LR2/61). Extensive extracts from it appear in Hope, *History of the London Charterhouse*. All major studies of the Charterhouse have used it, including G. S. Davies, *Charterhouse in London: Monastery, Mansion, Hospital, School* (London, 1921); D. Knowles and W. F. Grimes, *Charterhouse: The Medieval Foundation in the Light of Recent Discoveries* (London 1954); B. Barber and C. Thomas, *The London Charterhouse*, Museum of London Archaeology Service Monograph 10 (London, 2002); P. Temple, *The Charterhouse*, Survey of London Monograph 18 (New Haven, CT, 2010).

22 I. Grainger and C. Phillpotts, *The Cistercian Abbey of St Mary Graces, East Smithfield, London*, Museum of London Archaeology Monograph 44 (London, 2011).

23 D. S. Yocum, *Petrarch's Humanist Writing and Carthusian Monasticism: the Secret Language of the Self*, Medieval Church Studies 26 (Turnhout, 2013).

24 A. Wines, 'The Founders of the London Charterhouse', in *Studies in Carthusian Monasticism*, ed. Luxford, 61–71.

25 D. Knowles, 'The London Charterhouse', in *The Victoria History of the County of Middlesex*, I, ed. J. S. Cockburn et al. (London, 1969), 159–69.

26 J. Leclercq, 'Le cloître est-il une prison?', *Revue d'ascétique et de mystique*, XLVII, no. 188 (1971), 407–20.

27 Hope, *History of the London Charterhouse*, 56–7.

28 This *bulla* was originally attached to a papal licence (issued 1351) for Manny to choose his own deathbed confessor.

29 J. Luxford, 'The Space of the Tomb in Carthusian Consciousness', in *Ritual and Space: Proceedings of the 2009 Harlaxton Symposium*, ed. F. Andrews (Donington, 2011), 259–81.

30 Ode's will is in the Norfolk Record Office at Norwich. The document reference is Norwich Consistory Court, probate register Mouton, fols 34v–35v.

[31] Hope, *History of the London Charterhouse*, 41–6, 57–8.

[32] Walworth was Lovekyn's executor.

[33] Ibid., 55–104.

[34] The reed was, in effect, a metal drinking-straw, the use of which minimized the chance of spillage.

[35] Kew, The National Archives, document E315/490, fol. 22v.

[36] Hope, *History of the London Charterhouse*, 185–7.

[37] Retables and frontals are decorative panels, typically of stone, wood or cloth, fixed vertically to altars. A retable stands behind and above an altar's horizontal surface, a frontal before and below it.

[38] Hope, *History of the London Charterhouse*, 98.

[39] Ibid., 95.

[40] Kew, The National Archives, LR2/61, fols 104v–106v.

[41] This was very ably studied by Dr Andrew Wines in 'The London Charterhouse in the Later Middle Ages: an Institutional History', PhD thesis, U. Cambridge, 1998.

[42] These details come from ibid., chapter 4.

[43] London, British Library, MS Add. 11303, fol. 75v.

[44] N. R. Ker, *Medieval Libraries of Great Britain: a List of Surviving Books* (London, 1941, rev. 1964), 122–3. For the lists of lost books, see V. Gillespie and A. I. Doyle, eds, *Syon Abbey with the Libraries of the Carthusians*, Corpus of British Medieval Library Catalogues 9 (London, 2001), 614–29.

[45] Revised version of the Wyclif Bible, Oxford, Bodleian Library, MS Bodley 277.

[46] Another book of Henry VI's given to the Charterhouse is now at King's College, Cambridge (MS 4).

[47] London, British Library, MS Egerton 1821. Doyle's argument appears in an unpublished catalogue (kept at Durham University Library) of the manuscripts formerly belong to John Cosin, Bishop of Durham (d. 1672). Egerton 1821 was originally Cosin MS V III 23.

[48] The saga and its prelude are stirringly described in L. Hendriks, *The London Charterhouse, its Monks and its Martyrs* (London, 1889), 115–240.

[49] Kew, The National Archives, document E25/82/2.

[50] Knowles, 'The London Charterhouse', 167.

[51] Temple, *The Charterhouse*, 121–3.

[52] Kew, The National Archives, document E315/490, fol. 31.

Fig 28: **Decorative Tudor brickwork on the exterior wall of Wash-house Court**

Photograph by Lawrence Watson

E. Lutterell delin.   P. Vanderbanck sculp.

KING HENRY THE VIII.th

The Courtyard House

Stephen Porter

After the Dissolution the Charterhouse was not sold, unlike many other monastic properties, despite its size and desirable position on the fringe of London. It was administered by the Court of Augmentations, the body entrusted with the revenues and lands of the dissolved monasteries. Soon after the dissolution, Archibald Douglas, sixth Earl of Angus, was in possession of a part of the buildings, including five of the monks' cells 'nexte to the churche'. After his departure they were taken by Sir Marmaduke Constable, a member of the Council of the North.[1]

Constable's cells were among those later occupied by the five Bassano brothers, wind musicians from north-east Italy, who took cells Y and Z, the three new cells, the prior's new cell and the buildings around the east end of the church, together with five cells on the east side of the great cloister. The family, possibly of Jewish origin, had lived in Bassano del Grappa and later in Venice. One brother, Alvise, may have visited London in 1525 and he and three more came to England in 1531, although the duration of their stay is unknown. All five returned in the late 1530s and in 1540 at the invitation of the king. The recruitment of the brothers may have been intended to enhance the royal music consort in time for the anticipated wedding of Henry and Anne of Cleves, and her coronation. The terms for the marriage had been agreed by September 1539; Anne and her entourage arrived in England in late December and the wedding took place on 6 January 1540 at Greenwich. But the marriage was annulled in July and there had been no coronation, although it had been expected around Whitsuntide, which fell on 16 May, and was still being anticipated in early April.[2] Of course, the outcome of the marriage could not have been foreseen before Anne's arrival in England and Henry's reaction to her. Although the king may have instigated the moves to recruit the Bassanos, it is as likely that Thomas Cromwell initiated the process, as Henry's principal minister and the organiser of the Cleves marriage.[3]

The Bassanos were living in the Charterhouse before June 1542. The buildings were not conveniently located for the king's palace at Whitehall and the Charterhouse was the very place that had attracted attention because of the cruel treatment of its monks, but on the other hand it had some advantages. As it was extra-parochial it provided a residence beyond the parish system and so eased the immediate need to conform to the English church. It also offered physical security. The outer precinct was an enclosed space with gatehouses at its two entrances, and the inner precinct stood behind a wall with its own gatehouse, providing protection from crowds with malicious intent, if needed. Rioting in London was a rare event, but just over twenty years earlier, on May Day 1517, there had been violent disturbances directed at foreigners. It is likely that the Charterhouse was chosen with some care, as it provided a suitable group of buildings for the musicians during the process of assimilation into London.

In 1543 the remainder of the site was granted to John Bridges and Thomas Hale, respectively Keeper and Groom of the King's Halls and Tents, specifically for the safe keeping of the king's tents and pavilions. At the king's direction, the Charterhouse was divided between Bridges and Hale and the Bassanos.[4] When Henry returned from his campaign in France in 1544, during which Boulogne was captured, his tents and pavilions were stored at the Charterhouse in some of the church's side chapels and possibly also in the vestibule, where workshops were created and many people were engaged in repairing and maintaining the structures.[5] In 1545 the priory's flesh kitchen, in the outer precinct, and the granary were granted to John Bernard on his appointment as Clerk Comptroller of the king's tents, halls and pavilions 'and of the revels, masks and masking garments'.[6]

The costs of Henry VIII's wars with France and Scotland, from 1542, were so great that money was raised wherever possible and the Crown was obliged to sell much of the former monastic property.

Fig 29: **King Henry VIII, owner of the Charterhouse between 1537 and 1545.**

Engraving by Peter Vanderbanck (1649–1697).

Fig 30: Master's Court, the north range housing Lord
North's great hall.

In April 1545 Sir Edward North was granted the Charterhouse, the churchyard, the conduit head in Islington and the water pipes; shortly afterwards he was granted Bridges and Hale's interests, compensating them with an annuity of £10, and the king's pavilions and tents were removed to Sir Thomas Cheyney's house at Blackfriars.[7] A condition of his grant was that he should permit the Bassanos to continue to occupy their houses so long as they remained in the king's service. But he found their presence irksome, as he developed the property, and after Henry VIII's death in 1547 he tried to have them removed. They claimed that they had invested approximately £300 in the buildings and, although they were still at the Charterhouse in 1551, they had left by June 1552.[8] Despite the king's death and their expulsion from the Charterhouse, the Bassanos remained in London and prospered as musicians and musical instrument-makers.

North was the son of a London haberdasher and had trained as a lawyer at Lincoln's Inn. He attracted the attention of Sir Brian Tuke, Treasurer of the Chamber, and in 1531 he joined him as Clerk of Parliaments. Many of the duties of that office came to North and he also worked for Thomas Cromwell. In March 1539 he succeeded Sir Thomas Pope as treasurer of the Court of Augmentations. He was knighted in January 1542 and was well regarded by Henry VIII, who was to appoint him as one of his executors.[9] North had become a wealthy man and that, with his position at the Court of Augmentations, meant that he was well placed to pick this particular plum from the thirty-nine monastic properties in London.

North had ambitious plans for his new property. In the autumn of 1545 his workmen demolished large sections of the monastic buildings, including the priory church, the little cloister and the monastic cells, but they retained a number of other buildings, including the chapter-house, which was to become the chapel, and a long section of the west cloister walk. A mansion was then erected on part of the site, probably in the following year. His builders erected new ranges to form the principal courtyard of the new house (Hall Court, later Master's Court). The walls of the east range were built on the foundations of the earlier buildings and a substantial section of the west wall of the chapel of SS Michael and John the Baptist was retained and incorporated into the face of the new building. This is identifiable as an area of ashlar within the rubble-work.[10]

Around the principal courtyard were ranges containing a great hall and great chamber on the north side, a long gallery in the south range, and domestic quarters. The service buildings were retained, forming a smaller courtyard that was enclosed by the west range of North's new house. The inner arch, gatehouse and adjoining boundary wall were also retained.

The great hall occupies much of the northern range of Master's Court and is constructed of rubble-stone, with brick used for the heads above the three principal windows. A band of quatrefoils runs below the windows. Stone from the monastic church was used in the walls and the single buttress. Until the Second World War its roof carried a turret, destroyed in the fire in 1941 and not replaced. In its original form the great hall was open to the roof, with arched braces springing from the hammer-beams. The five hammer-beam trusses are moulded with geometric tracery in the spandrels containing quatrefoils and triskeles. On the pendants are cherub heads and foliage. A ceiling was added, almost certainly in the late Elizabethan or early Jacobean period, when longitudinal beams were attached connecting the ends of the hammer-beams, a plaster barrel vault was inserted springing from the new beams, and the spaces between the beams and the walls were filled with flat plaster ceilings.[11]

The upper storey on the north side of the great hall contained Sir Edward North's great chamber and its anteroom. By 1565 the great chamber was richly furnished with carpets and tapestries, and chairs

upholstered with cloth of gold and damask.[12] Beneath the great chamber, the monks' frater was incorporated into the new building, but the original form of this space is uncertain; it may have contained at least two rooms, one of them Lord North's closet.[13]

In 1565 the east range contained the dining chamber, two further chambers, neither furnished as bedchambers, and, at its south end, a bedchamber with an oriel window looking into Charterhouse Square and expressively designated the gazing chamber.[14] A long gallery occupied almost the entire first floor of the south range, providing a recreational space and means of communication between the side ranges, the ground floor being divided by the principal passageway into the court. (Long galleries were becoming fashionable in the 1540s, especially in the houses of courtiers.)

The kitchen was in the west range, where it adjoined the north range of Wash-house Court, with a spicery and a dry larder between it and the pastry kitchen. On the first floor, above the pastry kitchen, was Lord North's chamber, a large room with windows on to both Master's Court and Wash-house Court. By 1613 this room had become the privy chamber. The court that was formed by the three monastic ranges and the west range of the new court was referred to as Lavendry Court in the sixteenth century and later became known as Wash-house Court. The wash-house was in the south range.

On its east side the house encroached upon the south-west corner of the great cloister and a section of the cloister walk was converted into a bowling alley, while the greater part of the cloister garth was laid out as a formal garden. The new house continued to use the monastic water supply; monastic conduit house was demolished and a new one was erected in the garden or orchard on the north side of the wilderness, which was beyond the formal garden. This was close to the 'great brick wall' that separated the Charterhouse from the less salubrious property on its north side. The sites of the cells and their gardens on the west side

of the great cloister were cleared and the area was laid out as the privy garden. The cloister walk there, however, was retained and a gallery was built above it, which in 1565 contained a hanging measured at 336 square yards, so it must have been both enclosed and glazed.[15]

On the south side of the former great cloister, North retained the chapter-house and adjoining tower, but demolished the adjacent cloister walk, so that they were not linked to the house. It is likely that the chapter-house was adapted as its chapel, without the need for any structural changes. Its contents, listed in 1565, included ten long forms with desks, a table placed altar-wise, a lectern, a desk and a pair of regals. The more valuable items were in the wardrobe: richly decorated altar cloths of velvet, damask, satin and cloth of gold, one of them embroidered with angels and North's arms.[16]

Following the accession of Edward VI in 1547, North resigned from his post at the Court of Augmentations, though he continued as a Privy Councillor. In May 1553 he sold the Charterhouse to John Dudley, Duke of Northumberland, who perhaps envisaged it as a palace for his son Lord Guildford Dudley and his wife Lady Jane Grey. But Northumberland's plan that she should succeed Edward VI was swiftly defeated when Edward's elder sister, Mary, mobilised enough support to overturn Northumberland's infant regime and depose Queen Jane, who reigned for just nine days in July 1553. Following Northumberland's fall the Charterhouse came into the hands of the Crown, but North regained possession by Queen Mary's grant soon afterwards. He remained a member of the Privy Council during her reign and was created Baron North in 1554.

When Mary died on 17 November 1558 her sister and successor Elizabeth was at Hatfield House. She travelled to London a few days later and, arriving from the north, went directly to the Charterhouse, entering through the back gate to avoid the muddy streets. Her informality and lack of decorum in doing so were popular gestures.

Fig 31: The walls of the porch on the north side of Master's Court.

Photograph by Tom Hobson

Fig 32: **The great hall.**

Photograph by Tim Bruening

She stayed for five days before going to the Tower of London, and the early meetings of her Privy Council were held in the buildings, almost certainly in the great chamber. Elizabeth also visited North at the Charterhouse in 1561, accompanied by the court.[17]

In 1564 North negotiated the sale of the property to Thomas Howard, fourth Duke of Norfolk, but he died at the Charterhouse on 31 December and the transaction, which was to have been completed on 1 January, did not take place. Nevertheless, in a codicil to his will, made on the day before his death, North instructed that the sale should go ahead and the proceeds used to defray the debts of his eldest son and heir, Sir Roger North, who duly sold the Charterhouse to the duke in the following May for £2,200.[18] The sale included the conduit at Islington, with the water-pipes supplying the Charterhouse, and the gates of the outer precinct, which became designated Charterhouse Yard and later Charterhouse Square. During the Howards' ownership of the house, until 1611, with one interval when it was held by the Crown, the complex was known as Howard House, although it also continued to be called the Charterhouse, as indeed was the south-east part of the site retained by North in 1565, which in the seventeenth century became Rutland House.[19]

Norfolk was born in 1538 and succeeded his grandfather as Duke and Earl Marshal of England in 1554, his father having been executed for high treason in 1547.[20] As the only duke and first subject – he was descended from Edward I – he had a prominent position at court. The purchase of the Charterhouse gave him a second substantial mansion in London: through his second wife, Margaret, Lady Audley, he already had a house, Duke's Place, in Aldgate Ward, which her father had erected on the site of Holy Trinity Priory. His principal house was Kenninghall in Norfolk, and he had a substantial town house in Norwich, where he made extensive additions to the building erected by his grandfather. Although described by contemporaries as the richest man in England,

with an annual income estimated at £3,500, the duke's penchant for building works contributed to his indebtedness, as he admitted.[21] The queen paid a visit to the Charterhouse in January 1568 and in the following July stayed there, perhaps for almost a week.[22]

Norfolk was drawn into the complicated political manoeuvrings that followed Mary, Queen of Scots' flight from Scotland and arrival in England in the spring of 1568. She had a claim to the English throne, and Elizabeth was unmarried and without an obvious heir; there was, too, apprehension on the part of the English political elite that Mary may return to Scotland, in which case an English husband might be able to influence her policies. Norfolk was the obvious candidate, for he was close enough to the throne to be an acceptable consort for a queen, and he was a widower. The match may have been discussed before the end of 1568 and was certainly current in senior political circles by the following spring. Elizabeth was not informed, and indeed a part of the scheme was to topple William Cecil from his position as her leading adviser. The plotters were joined by Roberto Ridolfi, a Florentine banker who had dealings with Norfolk, but whose activities extended into international diplomacy. He was paid retainers by both the French and Spanish ambassadors, was an agent of the Pope in England and was widely connected with senior figures at Elizabeth's court. When Elizabeth discovered the scheme the plotters quickly disassociated themselves from it and Ridolfi left the country, but Norfolk had to explain himself. His involvement was regarded as foolish rather than treasonable and probably arose from frustration and resentment that he did not have as strong a role in government as was his due, but he was confined to the Tower and held there. The political landscape had been further complicated by a rising in the north of England in the autumn of 1569 and a Papal Bull issued by Pius V in the following year that proclaimed Elizabeth's excommunication and approved her deposition.

In August 1570 Norfolk was released but kept in virtual house arrest at Howard House. In the following January Ridolfi returned to England and promoted a new and more dangerous scheme, which again involved the marriage of Mary and Norfolk, but also a rising against Elizabeth supported by 10,000 troops from the Spanish Netherlands under the Duke of Alba. Elizabeth would be deposed and replaced by Mary, who would also regain her throne in Scotland, and Roman Catholicism would be restored. The duke conformed to the Church of England, but had Catholic connections, and his third wife had been a member of the Catholic Dacre family in the Scottish borders.

Norfolk had continued his correspondence with Mary throughout 1569 and 1570 and she now approached him reviving the marriage proposal; her representative John Lesley, Bishop of Ross, visited the duke at Howard House on a number of occasions. Ridolfi went there at least twice, holding discussions with him in the long gallery. On one occasion the duke's secretary described Ridolfi as using 'a new Payer of Stayers that goeth up to the old wardrobe' to meet the duke in the long gallery, which they reached through a chamber 'where my Lady Lestrange used to dine and suppe'.[23] They can be equated with a stair compartment and adjoining room to the west of the long gallery. Norfolk agreed to the proposed marriage and to head the planned rising, preparing either Portsmouth or Harwich for Alba's troops to disembark. Ridolfi, however, used the same cipher when exchanging letters with his English contacts and Gureau de Spes, the Spanish ambassador in England, and did not change it periodically, as prudent espionage practice would demand; he also sent unciphered letters to Mary. When the government intercepted Ross's correspondence and discovered what was going on, Norfolk's secretaries were interrogated and revealed what he knew. Howard House was searched and an incriminatory letter was found under a mat close to the duke's bedchamber. The key to the cipher in which it was written was discovered hidden between roof tiles.[24]

Norfolk was arrested in September 1571 and this time there was no escaping a charge of treason. He was tried in January 1572 by a court that consisted of virtually a half of the English peerage and was convicted. Elizabeth, though, was reluctant to send such a senior figure to the block and prevaricated for months before giving her consent to his execution, which took place on 2 June 1572. Ridolfi long outlived him, dying in Florence in 1612.

During the period when he was detained at Howard House between August 1570 and September 1571 the duke supervised a great deal of new work and alterations. Indeed, the years of his ownership mark the second major building phase of the house. That included the construction of the screen in the great hall, which is carved with the initials TN and the date 1571. Five bays wide, it is divided by fluted Corinthian columns on square panelled bases. The three centre bays contain enriched semicircular arches. In each bay the entablature is supported by console brackets decorated with lions' heads. The front of the minstrels' gallery above is now of four bays, the carved panels separated by pilasters carrying, alternately, male and female figures with bowls of fruit on their heads. The enriched cornice that projects over each of the figures was added by Edward Blore in the nineteenth century. The great chamber was redecorated during the duke's period, when the chimneypiece and ceiling were installed, and the projecting window bay in the north-west corner, an addition to the original structure, probably was built at that time. The west wall remained windowless until the nineteenth century. The work also included the insertion of a fireplace and imposing overmantel. The fireplace has a stone surround with a four-centred moulded arch set within a large and elaborately decorated architectural frame with two pairs of Doric columns. Most of Norfolk's plaster ceiling was destroyed in 1941. Only the small part within the window bay is original: the remainder is a replica made in the 1950s, incorporating some original elements. The ceiling is divided by moulded

Fig 33: **Details of the Tudor screen in the great hall.**

Photograph by Tom Hobson

gilt ribs and decorated by foliage and rampant lions. The square panels contain the Howard arms, the Howard crest and a lion rampant, and the side panels the motto *Sola virtus invicta*.

On the west side of the former great cloister the upper gallery was demolished to create an open terrace, which became known as the Queen's Walk, and the space beneath was vaulted to form the new cloister about 1571.[25] The cloister was an imposing feature, 263ft long, of which nearly a half remains, with a semicircular brick barrel vault. The west wall is the rubble-stone wall of the monastic cloister and the east wall is of brick, its piers coinciding with the positions of those of the monastic arcade, perhaps concealed beneath the brickwork. The east face was regularly fenestrated, broken by three canted bays; the one surviving bay has a corresponding shallower rectangular bay in the west wall that may have been intended for a seat. The cloister was plastered internally and glazed, containing 'divers maps & pictures' in 1608.[26] The outer faces have brick skins added in 1641. The cast-iron characters 'ANNO 1571' set in the west face refer to the building of the Norfolk Cloister, but it is unclear whether they were placed on the original outer face and transferred to the brick skin, or not put up until that was added.

The cloister and terrace provided a choice of walks, for inclement or fine weather respectively. Both overlooked the garden laid out on the site of the former great cloister, while the terrace also overlooked the privy garden, on its west side. By the early 1580s a tennis court stood on the west side of the Norfolk Cloister at its north end, probably erected as part of the duke's changes, and reached along the cloister. It was approximately 103½ft by 39ft, containing a large room shown in 1613 as 62ft by 32ft. The two-storey stair turret in the north-west corner of Master's Court is also likely to have been added as a part of Norfolk's changes, giving access to the privy chamber and the withdrawing chamber, and indirectly to the great chamber. (The third storey was added in the 1950s.) Towards the end of the sixteenth century John Stow

noted that Lord North and the Duke of Norfolk had erected 'large and sumptuous buildinges, both for lodging and pleasure'.[27] But Norfolk's programme of work perhaps was left unfinished after his arrest in September 1571.

On Norfolk's death the queen evidently waived the Crown's right to his estates, which should have been forfeit because of his treason, and the Charterhouse passed to his eldest son, Philip Howard (1557–1595), who held the courtesy title of Earl of Surrey – his father's title having been extinguished – until he succeeded his grandfather as Earl of Arundel in 1580. He lived there in the late 1570s until he inherited Arundel House in the Strand, and his wife Anne occasionally lodged in the Charterhouse.[28] At times it was let to tenants. Francesco Giraldi, the Portuguese envoy, occupied part of the buildings from 1573 until about 1578. The Elizabethan religious settlement in 1559 established the Protestant English church and over the following years those who persisted in following the 'old faith' became subject to increasingly harsh penalties. Yet conformity to the English church could not be enforced completely, despite penal fines imposed on those attending Roman Catholic services. Mass was celebrated in the private chapels of some country houses, and in London exception had to be granted to Catholic ambassadors and their retinues. But English citizens who attended mass at the embassies were not exempt from the law and in the spring of 1576 William Fleetwood, the Recorder of London (the City's senior law officer), wrote to Giraldi, warning him about the practice. This seemed to have no effect, and Fleetwood believed that on All Souls and All Saints days as many as two hundred English citizens went to mass at the Charterhouse. Accordingly, and perhaps at the suggestion of Cecil, who had been created Lord Burghley in 1571, he organised a raid early on a Sunday evening in early November.[29] Fleetwood and the two sheriffs arrived with their officers to arrest those English people who were at mass, which Giraldi and his household were attending in what

Fig 35: **The Norfolk Cloister.**

Photograph by Tim Bruening

Fleetwood described as 'a great long gallerie'. Sheriff Barnes went to the back gate, to prevent anyone escaping that way, while Fleetwood and Sheriff Kimpton demanded entrance at the gatehouse and entered only after a scuffle with the porter, who was 'a testy little wretche'.

Arriving at the long gallery, Fleetwood's party saw that 'all the masse-hearers, both men and women, were standing; for the priest was at the gospell, and the altar candells were lighted, as the old mode was'. All English subjects were ordered 'to come forth of that place'. This had an alarming effect, because 'then came all the straungers coming towards us, some of them beginning to drawe first their daggers, and then after they buckled themselfs to drawe their rapiers'. Kimpton reacted quickly by telling the strangers to be quiet and Fleetwood ordered two of his bailiffs who had drawn their swords to sheath them. But the throng kept coming so that, within moments, 'Mr. Kympton, with all the masse-hearers, with Mr Gerraldie's wife, and her maydes, were all in a heape forty persons at once speaking several languages'.

Fleetwood reduced the tension by politely leading the ambassador's wife by the hand to her chamber, and the other ladies from the embassy followed. Giraldi's retinue left, but only after 'many lewde and contumelious words used by them against us' and the other foreigners, who were not part of the embassy, also 'used such lewde wordes in theire language against us, that if our company had understande them, they might have chanced great harme'. Fleetwood threatened them with arrest and imprisonment, and then they quietened down and were allowed to leave. But Antonio Guaras stayed behind; he was the Spanish ambassador, but Fleetwood apparently was not aware of that at the time. The Englishmen left in the gallery were then questioned, to discover who they were, before being sent to prison. Fleetwood claimed that it was they who 'provoked the straungers into fury and disorder against us', because they were prepared 'rather to have murther committed than to be taken as they were'. When the officers

left Guaras accompanied them to the gate, but declined Fleetwood's invitation to dinner.

Of course, that was not the end of the matter. Both ambassadors complained to the queen and Fleetwood was summoned before the Privy Council. He claimed that he did not know that it was the ambassador's residence until the Privy Council told him, after the raid, and Kimpton excused himself by claiming that Fleetwood and others 'had commanded him to go thither'. So Fleetwood took full responsibility for the incident and, having despatched the Englishmen who had been at mass to prison, he was incarcerated there himself, to mollify the diplomats, but having done his penance for the queen's diplomatic embarrassment, he was soon released. In 1580 Portugal was absorbed into the Spanish dominions and did not regain its independence until sixty years later. The Charterhouse's period as an embassy had been brief, but not without drama.

The Charterhouse's association with Catholicism would not have been reduced by its next resident, Thomas Lord Paget, who was comfortably ensconced there by the early months of 1577 and may already have been there for some years.[30] Thomas was the son of William, first Lord Paget, a prominent figure in early Tudor government, and a landowner in Staffordshire. Thomas was mentioned in the Ridolfi papers as having Catholic sympathies. In August 1580 he was confined to a house in Windsor for several weeks while he was instructed by the Dean in the doctrine of the Church of England. Yet he was suspected of plotting on behalf of Mary, Queen of Scots; following the discovery of the Throckmorton plot, he fled to France in 1583, where he joined his brother William, who was acting as an agent for Mary.[31]

In the early 1580s Arundel's own political activities, especially his correspondence with Mary, aroused the government's suspicion. Following an unsuccessful attempt to leave the country without the queen's permission, in 1585 he was arrested and imprisoned. He was

attainted in 1589 and condemned to death, and, although the sentence was not carried out, he remained a prisoner for the rest of his life.

On Arundel's attainder the Charterhouse was forfeit to the Crown and between 1593 and 1595 a part of it at least was tenanted by the naval commander and privateer George Clifford, Earl of Cumberland (1558–1605). He, too, was brought up a Catholic in his early years, but was put under the tutelage of the Russell family in Hertfordshire, devout Protestants, and went on to Trinity College, Cambridge, where his tutor was John Whitgift, who was to become Archbishop of Canterbury. He took an MA in 1576 and showed an especial interest in mathematics, which may have led to a proficiency in navigation. At any rate, in 1586 he began a career as a privateer, perhaps in an attempt to recover his losses as a courtier and gambler. He took part in the naval campaigns against Spain in 1587 and 1588, including the Armada campaign, and then organised at least one privateering voyage each year over the next ten years, mostly in conjunction with syndicates of London merchants and with varying degrees of success. During one such voyage, in 1594, the great Spanish carrack *Cince Chagas* was captured, but lost after it caught fire; two of its officers may have been held at the Charterhouse until they were ransomed in 1595. [32] After a successful expedition in 1598 he withdrew from the privateering business and, although embarrassed by debts, returned to court, acting as the queen's champion. He posed in that role for Nicholas Hilliard, wearing her glove in his hat. [33]

Elizabeth restored the property to the Howard family in 1601, granting it to Philip's half-brother Lord Thomas Howard (1561–1626). Unlike Philip, Thomas had demonstrated his loyalty to Elizabeth and was created Baron Howard de Walden in 1597. The queen paid her final visit to the Charterhouse in January 1603, shortly before her death, when she was 'entertained and feasted'. [34] Doubtless in imitation of Elizabeth's arrival in London in 1558, and coached by Robert Cecil, who had overseen the succession, James I went directly to the Charterhouse when he reached the city in May and held court there. Elizabeth had been frugal in dispensing both money and honours, but in contrast James distributed his new-found wealth and authority quite freely and while at the Charterhouse he created 130 new knights. [35] That signified the change and provided encouragement for those who gathered at court like bees around a honeypot, hoping to attract royal favour, the enhanced status that gave and the wealth that could flow from it.

James was also generous with peerages and conferred the earldom of Suffolk on Thomas Howard in 1603 and converted Elizabeth's grant of the Charterhouse in fee-farm to an outright grant in 1604. The earl and his countess, Catherine, were enthusiastic builders who, between 1605 and 1614, constructed the vastly expensive prodigy house at Audley End and undertook extensive work at Charlton Park, Wiltshire, about 1607. It seems unlikely that they left no mark on their London house, and such important features as the great staircase and the ceiling and longitudinal gallery in the great hall may have been their improvements. They did not occupy the Charterhouse continually, however, and Dudley, Lord North – Roger, Lord North's grandson and heir – was their tenant there for a part of the first decade of the seventeenth century. [36]

On stylistic grounds the great staircase is likely to have been part of their changes, for the form and carved decoration of the arcaded balustrade and newel posts echoed the Jacobean staircases at Hatfield House and Blickling Hall. The staircase was in place by July 1608, when it was described as the 'great staires'; no other feature in the buildings would have attracted that description. It may have been constructed for the visits of Elizabeth or James in 1603, when Suffolk would have wished to impress his royal guests. The existing access to the great chamber and terrace walk was through the rather narrow stair compartment on the north side of the building, or indirectly from that added in the north–west corner of the courtyard about 1571. Neither provided a particularly dignified approach. During the conversion of the buildings in 1613–14 Thomas Sutton's

Figs 36, 37: **The Duke of Norfolk's motto and arms on the ceiling plasterwork in the great chamber.**

Photographs by Tom Hobson and Lawrence Watson

Fig 38: Thomas Howard, Earl of Suffolk, owner of the Charterhouse between 1601 and 1611. Painted by an unknown artist, 1598.

Reproduced by permission of the Weiss Gallery, London

Fig 39: Postcard showing the great chamber ('The Tapestry Room') around 1920.

Fig 40: Detail from an early seventeenth-century tapestry bought by the governors of Sutton's Hospital to furnish the great chamber.

Photograph by Lawrence Watson

greyhound crest was added to the face of the newel post between the flights; the greyhound finials, too, were probably later additions. [37]

The new compartment for the great staircase was created east of the anteroom and great hall. On the first floor it replaced the 'privy room', which did not have access to the anteroom of the great chamber, and so a new doorway was inserted, with the wall between the anteroom and the great hall cut back and its upper part carried on stone corbelling. A window at first-floor level in the west wall of the great staircase area provided a view into the great hall. This may have been associated with the 'privy room' at this level, which seems most likely, or it may have been inserted when the staircase was built. Such features were described by the seventeenth-century writer Donald Lupton as 'Peeping windowes for the Ladies to view what doings there are in the Hall'. [38]

The longitudinal gallery in the great hall provided a passageway between the first floor west of the hall and the 'privy room', or its replacement created for the great staircase. The new gallery greatly facilitated circulation at first-floor level in this part of the buildings, bypassing the great chamber and its antechamber. Tree-ring analysis has established that it cannot be earlier than 1607, while the absence of Thomas Sutton's insignia strongly suggests a date before 1611. [39] Twenty-two terms decorate the arcaded front of the gallery. Over every third term rises a tall tapering baluster with strapwork and an Ionic capital; beneath is an open scrolly pendant. The junction with the front of Norfolk's screen is crudely managed, the screen partially obscuring the carving of the term and baluster at the west end of the gallery.

The earliest house on that part of the site retained by North in 1565 was described two years earlier as having been newly built, perhaps by Sir Edward North, although that is uncertain. [40] It included a large two-storey structure with its gable fronting the square, two other substantial buildings on its east side and another behind them, abutting the Charterhouse's formal garden. When Roger, second Lord North,

died in the house in December 1600, the property passed to Dudley North, his grandson. [41] Although still a minor, Dudley claimed that his marriage, in November 1600, entitled him to occupy the house under the terms of his grandfather's will. [42] He moved in, but spent much of 1601 and 1602 with the English forces in the Netherlands and thereafter chiefly attracted attention for his extravagances at court. [43] From at least November 1602 Roger, fifth Earl of Rutland, was his tenant at a rent of £100 per annum and by 1608 Lord North's goods were in Howard House, which he held as the Earl of Suffolk's tenant, while the Earl of Rutland occupied North's house. Following Rutland's death in 1612, his brother and heir, Francis Manners, the sixth earl, apparently gave up the tenancy, but in 1630 he bought the house from Dudley, Lord North, and thereafter it was known as Rutland House. [44]

The transition from monastic to aristocratic occupation, when the priory was transformed into a mansion and a second aristocratic house, also saw the outer precinct evolve into a privileged enclave. The Charterhouse was the largest of a number of substantial houses erected here following the Dissolution, when courtiers were prominent among those acquiring buildings and land. Both the owners and occupiers within the precinct in the mid-sixteenth century were of high social rank, a characteristic that persisted until the late seventeenth century. Separate and secure, it was attractive because of its position at the edge of the city, yet beyond the authority of the corporation, and as a defensible area, with limited access along just two narrow streets guarded by gates.

References

1. William St. John Hope, *The History of the London Charterhouse from its Foundation until the Suppression of the Monastery* (London, 1925), 180; David Knowles and W. F. Grimes, *Charterhouse: The Medieval Foundation in the Light of Recent Discoveries* (London, 1954), 76–8.

2. *Letters and Papers, Foreign and Domestic, of the Reign of Henry VIII, 1509–47*, ed. J. S. Brewer et al. (London, 1862–1932), vol. 15, 1540, nos 401, 485.

3. David Lasocki with Roger Prior, *The Bassanos: Venetian Musicians and Instrument Makers in England, 1531–1665* (Aldershot, 1995), 3–11, 17–21, 92–7.

4. Kew, The National Archives, C4/8/1.

5. *Seventh Report of the Historical Manuscripts Commission*, appendix (London, 1879), 603.

6. *Letters and Papers of Henry VIII*, vol. 18/1, 1543, 548; vol. 20/1, 1545, 213.

7. London Metropolitan Archives, acc/1876/D1/4; *Documents Relating to the Office of the Revels in the Time of Queen Elizabeth*, ed. A. Feuillerat (London, 1908), 430–41.

8. *Letters and Papers of Henry VIII*, vol. 20/1, 1545, 303; Lasocki with Prior, *The Bassanos*, 20; Kew, The National Archives, C4/8/1.

9. P.R.N. Carter, 'North, Edward, first Baron North (c.1504–1564)', *Oxford Dictionary of National Biography* [*ODNB*] (Oxford, 2004).

10. Knowles and Grimes, *Charterhouse*, 57, 62.

11. Charterhouse Muniments [*CM*], B/1/7, 'The Roof of the Great Hall, Charterhouse'.

12. Philip Temple, *The Charterhouse*, Survey of London Monograph 18 (New Haven, CT, 2010), 199–200.

13. Ibid., 224–6.

14. Ibid., 203–4.

15. Ibid., 201.

16. Ibid., 222–3.

17. John Gough Nichols, ed., *The Diary of Henry Machyn*, Camden Society (London, 1848), 179–80, 263.

18. Kew, The National Archives, PROB/11/48. London Metropolitan Archives, acc/1876/D1/8.

19. London Metropolitan Archives, acc/1876/D1/10; Kew, The National Archives, E178/1396.

20. This and the following paragraphs are based on Neville Williams, *Thomas Howard, Fourth Duke of Norfolk* (London and New York, 1964); repr. as *A Tudor Tragedy: Thomas Howard, Fourth Duke of Norfolk* (London, 1989).

21. Ibid., 124–5.

22. Mary Hill Cole, *The Portable Queen: Elizabeth I and the Politics of Ceremony* (Amherst, MA, 1999), 183.

23. Gerald S. Davies, *Charterhouse in London: Monastery, Mansion, Hospital, School* (London, 1921), 137.

24. Geoffrey Parker, 'The Place of Tudor England in the Messianic Vision of Philip II of Spain', *Transactions of the Royal Historical Society*, 6th ser., XII (2002), 185–206, 215–17; Davies, *Charterhouse*, 135–41.

25. Kew, The National Archives, E164/45.

26. CM, M/9/19.

27. John Stow, *A Survey of London* (London, 1603); ed. C. L. Kingsford (Oxford, 1908), 83.

28. The Duke of Norfolk, *The Lives of Philip Howard, Earl of Arundel, and of Anne Dacres, His Wife* (London, 1857), 179.

29. For Fleetwood's account of the incident, see Thomas Wright, *Queen Elizabeth and her Times*, II (London, 1838), 37–41.

30. London Metropolitan Archives, acc/446/EF/25/11; Temple, *Charterhouse*, 50.

31. Peter Holmes, 'Paget, Thomas, fourth Baron Paget (c.1544–1590)', *ODNB*.

32. G. C. Williamson, *George, Third Earl of Cumberland (1558–1605)* (Cambridge, 1920), 132.

33. Peter Holmes, 'Clifford, George, third earl of Cumberland (1558–1605)', *ODNB*.

34. Sarah Williams, ed., *Letters Written by John Chamberlain during the Reign of Queen Elizabeth*, Camden Society (London, 1861), 174.

35. D. Harris Willson, *King James VI and I* (Oxford, 1956), 164.

36. *Calendar of State Papers, Domestic, James I, 1603–1610*, ed. Mary Anne Everett Green (London, 1857), vol. 2, 1603, 23; Kew, The National Archives, C54/1751/Dms Howard et Rex.

37. Royal Commission on the Historical Monuments of England, *London*, II: *West London* (London, 1925), 25.

38. D. Lupton, *London and the Countrey Carbonadoed and Quartred into Severall Characters* (London, 1632), 101.

39. R. E. Howard et al., 'Tree-ring Analysis of Timbers from the Great Hall of Charterhouse …', unpublished report, 1997.

40. London Metropolitan Archives, acc/1876/D1/19.

41. Kew, The National Archives, PROB11/97/6.

42. British Library, Add. MS 61,873, fols 15–16.

43. *The Complete Peerage*, 2nd edn, IX: *Moels to Nuneham*, ed. H. A. Doubleday and Lord Howard de Walden (London, 1932), 655–6.

44. Historical Manuscripts Commission, *Report on the Manuscripts of Lord Montagu of Beaulieu* (London, 1900), 114; CM,

Fig 41: **Detail from an early seventeenth-century tapestry bought by the governors of Sutton's Hospital to furnish the great chamber.**

Photograph by Lawrence Watson

Following pages:

Fig 42: **Master's Court.**

Photograph by Lawrence Watson

a day in the life of the Charterhouse

2: morning

	MORNING
9.00	Day staff and volunteers arrive.
9.00–12.00	Various activities: gardening; office work; cleaning and building repairs: Matron does her rounds in the infirmary; the day porter receives deliveries and signs in visitors; gardening staff and volunteers weed and plant; the archivist and curator catalogue the collection. Brothers read newspapers in the library, exercise, go shopping or entertain visitors. The residents who live in the rented flats on the site go about their business.
11.00	Start of public opening hours. The reception, shop, museum room and the Square's gardens are opened. School groups arrive.
11.30	Post arrives and is sorted into pigeonholes by a Brother.
12.00	Gardeners and maintenance staff have lunch in the old library.
12.00	A group of Brothers go to the pub before lunch (three times a week).

The Founder's Tomb

Nigel Llewellyn

When he died at his Hackney home on 12 December 1611, Thomas Sutton's great project to turn the Charterhouse from a patrician palace into the headquarters of a charitable organisation was still in development. Sutton had completed the legal and financial arrangements for his foundation but the finalising of the project as a whole was left in the hands of his successors. Despite the generosity of the bequest, the trustees and Sutton's executors faced great challenges to make real the founder's vision for a single institution that would both educate young boys and support a group of aged 'Brothers'. To make the vision real, support was needed from influential members of the early Stuart court, which is why one of the executors' pressing concerns must have been the immediate and longer-term handling of Sutton's public reputation.

As is made clear elsewhere in this collection of essays, he was a complex and controversial character, who by single-minded force of will had made not only a vast fortune but a good number of enemies, many of them through the money-lending business that he conducted so vigorously in the later years of his life. Despite being a painful necessity to borrowers, money-lending (or usury) was still tainted by a very long tradition of legal prohibition and moral condemnation and was, of course, one of the issues at the heart of Shakespeare's *The Merchant of Venice* (written in the very late 1590s). Usury had been legalised in 1570 providing that no more than 10 per cent interest was being charged on a loan. In deciding to commemorate Sutton as they did, by means of a grand wall-tomb erected on the north wall of the rebuilt Charterhouse chapel, the trustees were embarking on a carefully judged but quite risky endeavour. They had come to the view that the right kind of funeral monument would help to create a dignified, benevolent image for Sutton, one that stressed his virtues and charitable deeds, but they also had to ensure that they did not overreach themselves to create a perpetual image for their Founder that would claim too high a status

for him, something that might well have encouraged those who were dubious about the whole project. Indeed, the ideal tomb was one that would draw a discreet veil over some of Sutton's more questionable activities. So important were these various design agendas that, in commissioning a grand tomb, John Laws and his fellow trustees were also prepared to ignore Sutton's own clearly stated testamentary wish that he be buried and commemorated with modesty or, as he put it, without 'Pomp or Charge'.

In London at the start of the 1600s, when the Sutton tomb was made, standing wall monuments and other grand tombs were increasingly fashionable for well-to-do clients. The City churches were filling up with them as was St Paul's Cathedral in the City itself (destroyed in 1666). At the other great national mausoleum, the royal Abbey at Westminster, numbers of enormous tombs for courtiers were built in the apsidal chapels at the east end of the church, until the point was reached where all the space was in effect used up and patrons and tomb-makers had to start filling the transepts. Their great architectural height gave these monuments visibility and high status in those crowded spaces; their size was such that some complained that they shut out the light and blocked the view. English society about 1600 was intensely hierarchical and funeral monuments were expected to match their subject's social importance, which is why fears were sometimes voiced that especially grand monuments could be used by social climbers to give a misleadingly inflated impression of the individual's high status and so constitute a challenge to the natural order.

In the case of Sutton's tomb, there are five storeys in the architectural design. Working from the ground upwards, there is a basement to house the tomb-chest; above that an alcove flanked by columns to show off the monumental inscription; a third storey comprises a narrow frieze; then there is a square area flanked by more columns, which is for heraldry; and finally, there is the roof line adorned

Fig 43: **Thomas Sutton's monument in the chapel, installed in 1614.**

Photograph by Tim Bruening

SACRED TO THE GLORY OF G
MEMORY OF THOMAS SV

HERE LYETH ᵉVRIED Y BODY
LATE OF CA E CAMPES IN T
CAMBRIDGE AT WHOSE O
CHARGE PITALL WAS
ENDOWE GE POSSESSE
OF POORE HILDRē HEE
AT KNAYT OVNTY OF
THIE & HON PARENTAGE HE
OF 79 YEAR AND DECEASE

by sculpture. In its architecture, the tomb uses the standard repertoire of its day: free-standing and attached columns, ornamental panels, a kind of ornament popular at the time known as strapwork, pedestals and mouldings. Almost uniquely for a tomb of this date, we have very full records and accounts for the Sutton tomb – a direct consequence of the stability and continuity of the Charterhouse as an institution – and in an estimate dated 1613 we are told that a mixture of stones was to be used, all of it brought into London to be carved in the tomb-makers' workshops: nine loads of Midlands alabaster were used, at £6 the load; there was touchstone from the Low Countries, a more expensive commodity than alabaster; and rance (a type of stone) from the Rhineland. The document also tells us that most of the figure sculptures will cost between £3 (the smaller allegories) and £5 (the two 'Captains' and the larger allegories).

The architecture of the Sutton tomb frames more than one kind of sculpture, although none of the scale relations between the carved figures are at all realistic. With the exception of Sutton's effigy, we are presented here with a fictional cast of characters; with the exception of the low-relief panel in the frieze, the carvers are not depicting scenes from real life. Sutton's contemporaries would have started any description of the sculpture with his effigy, which shows him in an entirely orthodox pose, as an old man, lying recumbent on a tomb-chest, dressed in a long, warm, fur-lined robe, facing the east in the expectation of resurrection and with his hands clasped in prayer. The effigy was to cost £10, although this includes an heraldic supporter at Sutton's feet, which was never carved. The estimate was drafted by experienced tomb-makers, who must have assumed that there would be an heraldic supporter of some description and therefore included a carving of one in the price. The herald's choice of the greyhound as supporter either came too late for inclusion in the carving of the effigy, which was all carved from one block, or the

tomb-makers had simply used up the budget by the time the herald made his decision. Behind and above Sutton, on the back wall of the alcove created by the large touchstone columns, are two standing figures identified in the contractual documents as 'Captains' or military leaders. These are swaggering bravos, tough-looking military men guarding the monumental inscription. Behind them, reclining on the frame of the inscription panel itself, is a winged skull and an hourglass. These allegorical sculptures are signalling to the onlooker that there is no time to be lost, 'Death might strike at any moment', 'The sands are always running out!' This imagery is juxtaposed, rather uncomfortably, with two other standard symbols of the memento mori tradition that had existed in English art for centuries. To the right is a figure representing Chance, with his scythe, showing his tendency randomly to destroy things that he happens upon and, with his prominent forelock, signalling that chance has to be grabbed as it passes by. To the left is Vanity, shown here as a winged boy blowing bubbles to symbolise the fragility of earthly life. This old man and young boy must have been a gift to any preacher in the chapel seeking to reach either of the key groupings in any Charterhouse congregation, namely, the young scholars who needed to be reminded of the dangers of worldly vanity and the old brethren likely to fall victim to Chance's scythe at any moment.

On the higher levels of the monument there is a troop of nine smaller, free-standing sculptures, some of them little naked boys, or putti, but five depicting draped, mature female figures. By convention in European art at this time, female figures of this kind do not represent historical individuals but abstract concepts, in this case the particular virtues of the individual commemorated. Amongst these allegorical personifications, Charity is given pride of place, dominating the uppermost register and flanked by two trumpeting figures of Fame. Here we have the strongest possible signal of the

Fig 44: **The figure of a 'Captain', from Sutton's monument, probably representing Sutton's service to the Army.**

Photograph by Tom Hobson

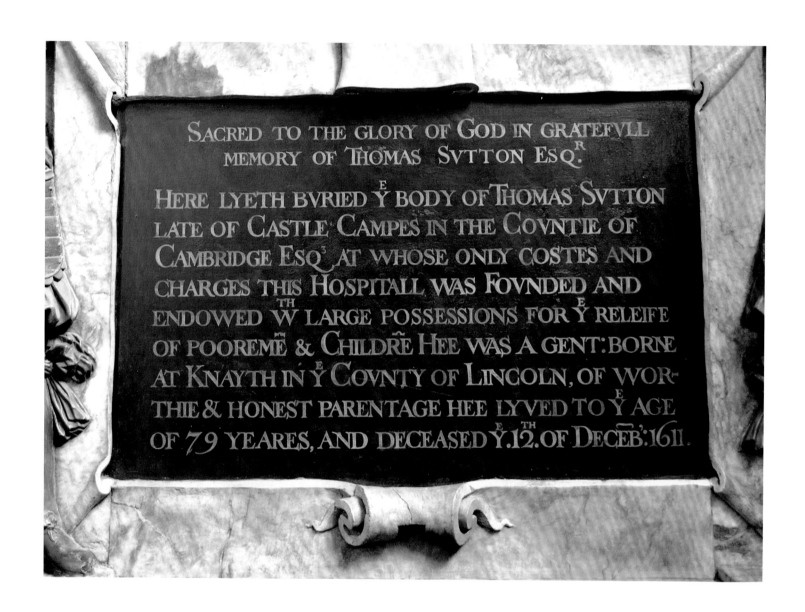

Fig 45: **The inscription on Sutton's monument.**

Photograph by Tom Hobson

primary purpose of Sutton's monument, the perpetuation of his charitable donation. On the level below there are six more figures, three on each side; to the right (the liturgical east) stands Faith holding a book of scripture behind a cherubic boy with an inverted torch and skull, who is Rest, that is, the rest from physical labour that death represents. Above them is a figure probably representing Piety, reminding us that religious instruction was high on the curriculum for the occupants of Sutton's new institution. To the left (the liturgical west side) stands Hope with her anchor behind Rest's twin brother, who is of course Labour with his gravedigger's shovel. Behind and above them is Bounty or Wealth, signified by the cornucopia out of which natural treasures spill. The prominence of Faith, Hope and Charity amongst the virtues reminds us of the emphasis given those qualities by St Paul, such an important scriptural source in post-Reformation England. Figures like these semi-naked matrons, who were pagan in origin, were not entirely uncontroversial in the 1610s: John Weever, writing in 1631, criticised 'their fantasticke habits and attires, which in time to come will rather be provocations to vice, then incitations to vertue'.

What is more like real life than any of these allegorical figures is the final piece of sculpture, the remarkable low-relief panel that fills the frieze over the canopy in the very centre of the monument. This panel, called a 'storye' in the accounts, was to cost £10, the same price as the effigy, which suggests that it was evidently an important part of the overall programme. A sculptural narrative showing the new foundation at work seems always to have been part of the patron's vision. But when the piece was commissioned the charity had not yet been set up, its quotidien working pattern and character had still to be established and could not yet be witnessed. Instead the sculptor has had to create an idealised depiction of the kind of pious instruction that he imagines will be part of everyday life at the Charterhouse. The relief panel shows

the preacher standing in a pulpit, amongst his congregation of forty brethren who appear to be listening intently but who are depicted without much individuation, since no individual had yet been admitted. The Brethren are shown as orderly and respectful in their demeanour, neatly arranged on either side of the preacher, whose elevated position indicates his special status and whose hand gestures signal that he is speaking. The scene shows the preaching of the Word to the people in full accordance with Protestant orthodoxy. To the sides onlookers stand about in pairs and small groups. Given their costume, appearance and manner – not unlike the 'Captains' but without the armour – we can assume that the carver is portraying Sutton's trustees, the governors of his foundation, members of the courtier class and exactly the same kinds of people that the sculptor of the scene, Nicholas Stone the Elder, would work for over the next thirty or so years.

In addition to the architectural frame and the effigial and subsidiary sculpture, there are two other aspects of the monument that need to be noted. First is the inscribed text. Some monuments of this type are covered in words – Biblical quotations, didactic mottoes, heraldic captions, genealogies, names and initial letters. But Sutton's monument displays just one framed inscription, written in English – the alternative would have been Latin – which gives a simple account of the occupant. It reads:

Sacred to the glory of God in gratefull / memory of Thomas Sutton, Esquire / Here lieth the body of Thomas Sutton / late of Castle Camps in the county of / Cambridge Esquire at whose only costs and / charges this hospital was founded and / endowed with large possessions for the relief / of poor men and children he was a gentleman / born at Knayth in the county of Lincoln of wor / thy and honest parentage He lived to the age / of 79 years and deceased the 12th of December 1611.

This text is interesting but, in comparison with so many contemporary monumental inscriptions, it offers very little on Sutton's ancestry ('a gentleman') or his patrons, and the biography is sketchy with very few dates. There is no family history or career history and there is nothing on his education. Sutton's wife – on whom the monument is completely silent - was Elizabeth, the widow of one John Dudley, a distant cousin of the earls of Warwick and Leicester, the former of whom in 1569 secured for Sutton the post of Master of the Ordnance, that is, the supplier of military armaments and artillery to the army stationed in the North (the Scottish border). It was the leases that came with that position that allowed Sutton to control the mines from which he derived his enormous wealth, worth millions if not billions of pounds by today's reckoning, which was then used on the London money markets. The many absences in this inscription are, in fact, clear indications of the challenge that Sutton's trustees faced. The reputation of the great philanthropist had to be carefully stitched together. Telling the complete story in candid language would have brought poor publicity and have done little to meet the patrons' intention or support their charitable cause.

Finally, there is the heraldry, in the form of a splendidly carved display in the upper section of the monument. Heraldry was of enormous significance in Sutton's day and we ignore it at our peril. To have a coat of arms was a condition to which all socially ambitious individuals aspired and there was a complicated science and institutional bureaucracy dedicated to the business of designing, granting and interpreting heraldic signs. In this case, we have what was called an achievement-of-arms, that is, a shield of arms displaying signs, adorned with lavish, feathery, acanthus-like stuff and topped off by a knightly helmet and a greyhound's head, this last being the heraldic supporter, which on other monuments of this type and date we might also have expected to see on guard at the effigy's feet. What is especially interesting in relation to the Sutton arms is the fact that they were not granted in his lifetime, something that concerned the trustees when they commissioned the tomb. They knew that a monument without heraldry would be thought lacking in dignity. As we have just read, the monumental inscription refers to Sutton's title as Esquire, the lowest rank in Jacobean heraldic etiquette, which would permit him to bear arms or to be armigerous, to use the Jacobean term. An heraldic display was a prerequisite in the creation of a dignified monument, which meant that a coat of arms had to be adopted for Sutton after his death. In answer to the executor's request, the necessary work was done by the most prominent herald of the day, William Camden, who occupied the post of Clarenceaux King-at-Arms and who came up with the solution that we see displayed on the tomb in a heraldic formula that included the greyhound's head, also prominently displayed elsewhere in the chapel, including on the monument's original protective wrought-iron grille. Camden – ever the pragmatist – simply borrowed the blazon of another Lincolnshire family called Sutton.

During the medieval period, when the palace was a monastery under Carthusian rule, it is recorded that the Charterhouse had been well connected to the fashionable and political elites; and it remained so during the short period between the acquisition of the ex-monastic property by Sir Edward North in 1545 and its sale to Sutton in 1611. In these years, even when the house had been a centre of Elizabethan Catholic dissent, it was never isolated from secular power and this tradition continued as Sutton's new foundation was being established in the old buildings. The great and the good were not only on the board of governors, but as we have seen, they are referenced on the monumental low relief and shown there to be moved to prayer and reflection on the meaning of the divine message. This carved 'storye' is amongst the first of its type in this country and it signals the increasing interest in post-Reformation monuments that create

Fig 46: **Detail from Sutton's monument: the figure represents the ephemeral nature of Time.**

Photograph by Lawrence Watson

fictional accounts of the individual's virtues and, in an adaptation of the Florentine Renaissance theory expounded by writers such as Alberti, can provide an exemplary function for spectators. The function of historical or narrative art such as the Charterhouse 'storye' was to be didactic, to show onlookers how good people behaved and to set out the virtues of exemplary individuals such as the enlightened philanthropist and reformed usurer Thomas Sutton. Isaac James, who was the master of the key tomb-maker at Charterhouse, Nicholas Stone, is associated with narrative low-relief carvings like this, such as the ambitious reliefs on James's monument to the soldier Lord Norris, which was erected in Westminster Abbey about 1611. Furthermore, it is certain that this was also an aspect of tomb-making that Stone had carefully noted during his long stay in the Netherlands before returning to London to seek commissions. One interesting parallel was spotted by Stephen Porter at Enkhuizen on the front of an orphanage built in 1616.

Between his death and his final committal in December 1614, Sutton's body was first moved to the house of his executor, the lawyer John Laws, on Paternoster Row just by St Paul's Cathedral. Here an apothecary treated the body and encased it in a lead coffin. It was then buried temporarily in nearby Christchurch, Newgate Street. The coffin was of an anthropomorphic type and was inscribed with Sutton's name and death date. When it was rediscovered under the chapel floor in 1842 a plaster cast of it was taken as a record. This kind of coffin is a sure sign that the trustees planned elaborate rituals for Sutton right from the start. They had the body encased in lead in the knowledge that elaborate public funerals needed time to organise and meanwhile the natural processes of bodily corruption needed to be managed. Even before his death, in fact, on 19 July 1611, the governors had ordered that there should be a Founder's tomb and that it should be placed on the north side of the chapel alongside the scholars' seats.

Fig 47: Portrait of Thomas Sutton, engraved by Frederick Hendrik van Hove (c.1628–1698) as the frontispiece to Samuel Herne, *Domus Carthusiana: or, an account of the Most Noble Foundation of the Charter-House ...* (London, 1677).

But it took time for the space needed to be made ready. The south aisle of the present chapel, leading up to the altar, had been transformed out of the medieval chapter-house by the first set of post-Reformation owners, the Norths, in the 1540s. As was usual in great houses at this date, North's chapel was a domestic place for worship within private premises: it was not a church. Furthermore, the family did not need the Charterhouse chapel for commemorative purposes, committing instead to the church at Kirtling, Cambridgeshire, adjacent to their manorial seat. Equally, their successors at Charterhouse, the Howards, Dukes of Norfolk, were committed to their long-established mausoleum at Framlingham and the Earl of Suffolk, who sold the Charterhouse to Sutton, had been thoroughly distracted by his rebuilding of Audley End, the great house near Saffron Walden. About sixty-five years after the monks left, however, when those responsible for the new foundation were estimating how the Charterhouse complex would suit its future needs, the chapel that had been created by Lord North from the south aisle alone was judged too small and the governors, mindful as they were of the requirement to encourage piety amongst the young scholars and the older brethren, decided to enlarge the space by building a second parallel aisle immediately to the north of it. To this end, the original north wall was removed and replaced by an arcade. This arcade is a rare example of Jacobean ecclesiastical architecture and was designed by Francis Carter. It is close to a similar work by him at Hatfield intended to accommodate a monument for the Earl of Salisbury. At Charterhouse, the newly occupied space was taken from the old cloister – in fact, Lord North's bowling alley – which had run alongside but outside the original chapter-house wall. Initially it was planned that the new north wall would have three substantial windows looking out into the garden. By the time it was finally built, however, only two of these were installed since by then the decision had been taken to install the founder's monument in this newly enlarged space, in

the north-east corner of the chapel and where the third window would have been. The chapel had been made bigger both to accommodate a larger congregation and to create a space where the foundation's rituals could be enacted. Not only was a founder's tomb commissioned but also a grand pew was installed from which the Master could preside. The semi-public space of the newly enlarged Charterhouse chapel was the context that Stone had in mind when he was designing and cutting his low-relief scene and carving the allegorical figures. The only substantial additional change to the chapel came more than 200 years later in the 1840s when an east window was punched into the north aisle alongside Sutton's monument, and the chapel was enlarged still further to the north to provide even more seating.

On 12 December 1614, exactly three years after his death, Sutton's coffin was carried at night – a not uncommon practice at the time – on the shoulders of some of the more robust pensioners in a torch-lit procession from Christchurch to Charterhouse, where a funeral oration was pronounced over the body prior to it being committed in the newly constructed vault in the north-east corner. Sutton was finally laid to rest under the present monument, which was by then being made in the workshop to be brought into the building and set up no later than the November of the following year, 1615.

We know a good deal about the authorship of the monument from the surviving contractual documents and also from an entry in a notebook kept by Nicholas Stone himself: 'In November 1615 Mr Janson in Southwark and I did set up a tombe for Mr Sottone at Charter hous for the wich we had £400 well payed … [and] I mad … all the carven work of Mr Sottons tombe.' In fact, Janson (or Jenson and now known as Johnson), who flourished between 1594 and his death in 1624, and another mason called Kinsman (a citizen and freeman of London and active between 1613 and 1643) had secured the initial commission with Johnson intending always to supply the architectural parts of the

monument. They then subcontracted the sculpture to the young and newly emerging master carver Nicholas Stone, who had recently arrived back in London after a period working in the Netherlands. So, as is the case with so many works of this kind, the Sutton tomb was a collective enterprise. Kinsman was employed elsewhere on the site, making the decorative entrance doorway to the chapel and the ceremonial gateway into the Charterhouse burial ground, on the north-west side, which was itself decorated with memento mori motifs and funerary urns. Kinsman's and Johnson's were the original signatures on the contract of 1613, signed a year or so after Sutton's death. The second of these. Nicholas Johnson, is relatively well known and his career typifies tomb-making in Jacobean London. His father Garret Jansen had arrived in England in the 1560s – note that Stone, who would have known this history and who also knew Holland, still called Nicholas by his Dutch name Janson, rather than Johnson – and he represents the transition from the Elizabethan trade dominated by Netherlanders to the greater stylistic and iconographic diversity of the seventeenth century. Nicholas Johnson had a long career, supplying the social elite with large complex monuments, many of them erected in churches attached to landed estates but also in the key commemorative sites of Westminster Abbey and Old St Paul's, spaces which were steadily becoming showcases for what was an increasingly competitive trade on the sculptor's part and a kind of ritualised competitive performance on the parts of the subjects and patrons, who were vying with one another to build the most splendid monument. Johnson was the heir to his father's business, which is why he himself referred to his late father Garret in an estimate that he wrote for the Charterhouse commission. All these makers tended to take on subcontracts and split contracts, sharing commissions with other makers and workshops in a series of short-term partnerships. In the case of the Charterhouse monument, Johnson's initial partnership was only with the stonemason Kinsman, of whom there is no record

Fig 48: **Thomas Sutton's crest, the head of a greyhound, carved on a pew in the chapel.**

Photograph by Lawrence Watson

that he was ever actually engaged in carving monuments. After a time, it was felt that the project would benefit from another set of skills being brought in, hence the involvement of Nicholas Stone, born in the mid-1580s, who was to become the greatest tomb-maker in Jacobean and Caroline England until his death in 1647.

Stone is cited in the later documents for the Sutton tomb, namely receipts for payment dated May and November 1615. As is often the case in these transactions, there are some points of difference between the estimate and the finished monument. For example, the 1613 estimate describes the two 'Captains' as 'sitting', whereas in fact they stand on the finished tomb and there are discrepancies between the estimate and the actual number of 'pictures' (the statues set up on the upper reaches of the monument). Nicholas Stone was a much younger man than Johnson; he was a Devonian and, as his name suggests, the son of a quarryman from near Exeter. It was Nicholas Stone's apprenticeship in London to the distinguished Low Countries sculptor Isaac James that transformed his prospects. James's ancestors had also come to England in the reign of Henry VIII and by 1600, when he is first documented, he was well established in London. He was still living in the mid-1620s in the parish of St Martin-in-the-Fields, then on the western fringes of the metropolis and fast becoming a major centre for tomb production. This is in contrast with Nicholas Johnson, whose headquarters were in Southwark, at Bankside, in the area originally frequented by his father and by the 1610s starting to become something of a backwater. Nicholas Stone spent three years with James as apprentice and journeyman and then in 1606, through James, he met Hendrick de Keyser, the most important master stone carver then practising in Amsterdam, who was making a visit to London. Perhaps sensing his rare talent, de Keyser took Stone back to the Netherlands where he stayed for a number of years; he returned to London in early 1613, the proud possessor of gifts that would stay with him for the rest of his career. The first gift was

artistic: Nicholas saw innovative work in the Netherlands and learned to use sculptural motifs that entered his repertoire never to leave it; secondly, he made invaluable business contacts, becoming not only a top-rank carver but a successful merchant in the import and export of fine, sculptural stones, a business that his sons continued after him. The final gift was that on 14 May 1613 Nicholas Stone married Mayken (or Mary) de Keyser, his Dutch master's daughter, and they settled in the parish of St Martin-in-the-Fields.

Nicholas Stone came into the reckoning for Sutton's tomb quite late in the day since he was living abroad when the project was first being discussed. The commission gave him the chance to show his clients, the governors and the other visitors to the Charterhouse, what he was capable of and allowed him to publicise to a London audience some new ideas about tomb-making, particularly the use of elegant allegorical figures and the didactic and narrative possibilities of low-relief scenes. Although Stone was aged only about 25 at this time, the episode also suggests that an astute businessman was at work. When the final bill for the monument was settled, it cost Sutton's executors £400 rather than the £366 that had been contracted before because Stone pulled one last trick. The partnership supplied not only the Sutton monument, as agreed, but also a small monument to commemorate John Laws, Sutton's executor and therefore the patron of the Sutton tomb itself, who had died unexpectedly in October 1614, aged 61, in the middle of the project. Laws was buried and commemorated over the door at the east end of the south aisle in the Charterhouse chapel. Stone made his small monument and it comprises a portrait bust in an oval niche, the frame of which is supported by two remarkable ethereal, armless, allegorical figures. Above is a boy blowing bubbles, astride a skull, the twin of the Sutton Vanitas figure, an appropriate choice given that Law had died without much warning. In offering to add to the Sutton contract a monument

Fig 49: **Seventeenth-century carved head on the organ screen in the Chapel.**

Photograph by Lawrence Watson

to the late lead executor, Stone was making an offer that was impossible for the other executors to refuse and was also cementing his place in the partnership for the larger commission.

In conclusion, it is clear that Sutton's executors needed a monument but its design had to be very carefully judged. They had to make sure that their monument would not look vainglorious and that the spending was legitimate. The Sutton tomb was by no means cheap – the final cost of £400 for materials and labour represented four years of the salary of the Foundation's supervising architect/surveyor, Francis Carter – but it does not gloat and it does not show off. It emphasises the key virtues of the mere commoner Sutton as being piety and charity. He is given the lowest rank of heraldic status to add dignity to the tomb, but a veil is drawn over aspects of his career and scandal is thereby avoided. Care was taken that the founder would not appear self-aggrandising or self-promoting; to have misjudged that would have been to throw the executors open to accusations of idolatry. The tomb makes a legitimate monumental display of Sutton's status without overclaiming his social degree. The patrons knew that they had to take care to match the kind of person to the type of monument that they had erected, a major issue at the time when, as the earlier quotation from Weever demonstrates, there were complaints that mere tradesmen were having themselves entombed like lords.

Sutton's monument is carefully designed to meet its unique circumstances and the design brief has been brilliantly carried out. It commemorates a particular set of virtues and it teaches onlookers how they too should behave: be pious, be charitable and prepare for your own end. The tomb both invents and presents a history and has an active didactic role in the lessons it teaches. Compared to some contemporary monuments it is relatively restrained: it does not show off by means of endless biographical accounts of achievements or posting up lists of fictitious ancestors, and it does not crow about the offices that its subject held in life. What the Founder's tomb tells us is that Sutton should be remembered as a man of modest social rank but also a man of piety and virtue, whose fame lies in the good he has done by using his great wealth to provide for future generations. Whatever the truth about Sutton's character, his executors and the tomb-makers did well.

A NOTE ON SOURCES

The ideas in this essay were originally presented in the form of a lecture, given at the Charterhouse in February 2012. A number of people gave me valuable guidance in its preparation, in particular, Stephen Porter, the charity's honorary archivist, and Sue Lee, who conserved the monument. For a thorough and sympathetic treatment of the history of the built fabric of the London Charterhouse, see Philip Temple, *The Charterhouse*, Survey of London Monograph 18 (New Haven, CT, 2010). The tomb-makers involved in the commission for the Founder's tomb are well documented by Adam White, 'A Biographical Dictionary of London Tomb Sculptors, c.1560–c.1600', *Walpole Society*, LXI (1999), 1–161. For the rich documentation on the monument itself, see Gerald S. Davies, *Charterhouse in London: Monastery, Mansion, Hospital, School* (London, 1921). John Weever's *Ancient Funeral Monuments* (London, 1631) is a rich source of near-contemporary comment on monuments, the wider context of which is described in Nigel Llewellyn, *Funeral Monuments in Post-Reformation England* (Cambridge, 2000). For Sutton himself, see Hugh Trevor-Roper's entry in the *ODNB* and John Aubrey, *Brief Lives*, ed. Richard Barber (London, 1975), 295–6.

Fig 50: **Thomas Sutton's arms, carved on the organ screen in the chapel.**

Photograph by Lawrence Watson

Thomas Sutton's Hospital

Stephen Porter

Thomas Sutton was born in 1532 and so was an elderly man when he died on 12 December 1611, with the reputation of being the richest commoner in England. His great wealth naturally attracted envy and anxious concern on the part of those who hoped to benefit from his fortune, which had been accumulated from his service with Richard Cox, Bishop of Ely (1559–81), for whom he may have acted as under-steward, and the brothers Robert Dudley, Earl of Leicester, and Ambrose Dudley, Earl of Warwick. It was through the Dudleys' influence that he was appointed in February 1570 as Master of the Ordnance in the North Parts. He held the post until 1594, although he stayed in the north of England only until 1582. Such an appointment did not preclude the holder from private dealing, and Sutton engaged in trade on his own account. More profitably, he obtained, again through Leicester's influence, a lease of coal mines in County Durham, formerly part of the Bishop of Durham's estates, which he sold in 1583 for £12,000. On his return to the south it was said that he carried two horse-loads of money with him. He then made an advantageous marriage, to Elizabeth Dudley, the widow of John Dudley of Stoke Newington, a distant cousin of Leicester and Warwick.[1]

In his later years Sutton increased his assets by lending on mortgages and recognisances, which carried an annual rate of interest of 10 per cent. In the last sixteen years of his life he lent £220,000, with £37,000 advanced in 1604 alone.[2] After his wife's death in 1602 he sold the house at Stoke Newington and bought one at Hackney, but did not invest in property in London, preferring to accumulate country estates, especially in Cambridgeshire, Suffolk and Essex, and he regarded Castle Camps in Cambridgeshire as his country seat. When he was in London he lodged in rooms above a shop in Fleet Street.

Curiosity concerning his financial planning was further increased following his wife's death. He had an illegitimate son, Roger Sutton, but did not give him financial support after 1592. Yet as early as 1595 he had prepared a draft will providing for the endowment of a hospital, chapel and school at Little Hallingbury in Essex. He subsequently developed the plans, adding considerably to the proposed endowment and examining the procedures followed in the setting up of similar charitable institutions. He then obtained an Act of Parliament for the purpose, in 1610, but in the following year acquired the Charterhouse, which had special significance through its connection with both Elizabeth I and James I. As the Act of 1610 referred to Little Hallingbury, Sutton now obtained Letters Patent, which were issued on 22 June 1611, establishing the charity.[3] They specified that the Charterhouse was to house the foundation, with the name 'The Hospital of King James, founded in Charterhouse within the County of Middlesex'.[4] By honouring the king he hoped to secure his support should the plans be challenged.

To further ensure that avaricious courtiers or other predators did not thwart his plans and divert the endowment to their own benefit, Sutton appointed as governors some of the most powerful men at the heart of the Jacobean establishment: high-ranking clergymen and lawyers with the knowledge and authority to carry out his plans and protect his legacy. The sixteen governors included six clergymen, including the Archbishop of Canterbury and the Bishops of London and Ely, and eight lawyers, including the Lord Chancellor, the Chief Justice of the Common Pleas and the Attorney General. The Earl of Salisbury, Lord High Treasurer, was also made a governor, as were Sutton's executors, John Law and Richard Sutton. Law died in 1614, leaving Richard Sutton to collect the residue of the debts and income from the estate; he continued in that role until 1629.

Almshouses and schools were conventional outlets for a philanthropic gift on the scale that Sutton was able to provide. The elderly in need and the children of the poor were regarded as the most deserving sections of society, and their foundation was one of the major forms of charitable giving by wealthy philanthropists. Sutton's charity

Fig 51: **Chair from the Charterhouse, age unknown.**

Photograph by Tom Hobson

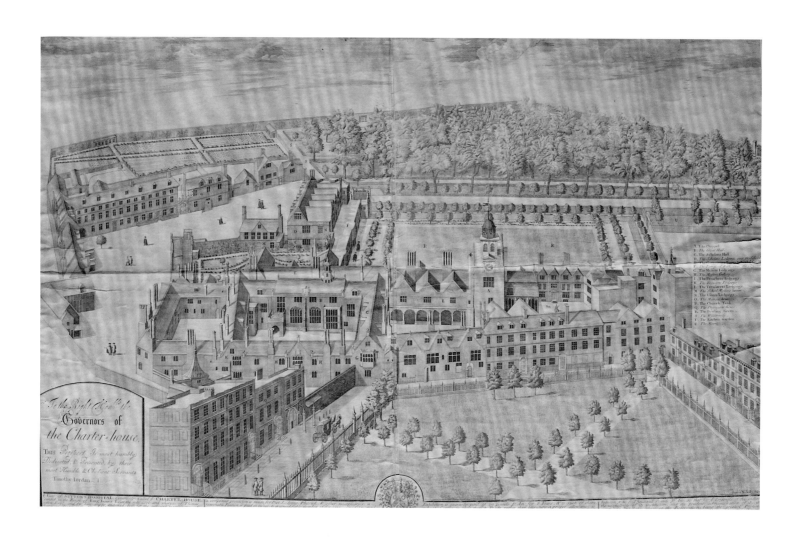

Fig 52: A large panorama of Sutton's Hospital engraved for the governors around 1720 by Sutton Nichols.

was remarkable because of the choice of an aristocratic mansion to house the institution and the scale of the endowment, which was the largest investment in a private charity in London between the Reformation and the founding of Guy's Hospital in the 1720s. The number of pensioners was set at eighty and the number of scholars at forty; and the governors added a third element by providing exhibitions for boys from the school at university. By 1628 there were twenty-six exhibitioners at the two universities; the number fluctuated from time to time, depending on the charity's income, which was chiefly from land in Clerkenwell, Cambridgeshire, Huntingdonshire, Essex, Devon, Yorkshire, Lincolnshire and Wiltshire.[5] The governors had to deal with a claim from both Sutton's illegitimate son, Roger, and fight off legal challenges to his will, the most serious of which was from his heir Simon Baxter. Because of the delays that they caused and the need to adapt the buildings, the pensioners and scholars did not move in until October 1614.

Soon after buying the Charterhouse Sutton appointed Francis Carter as surveyor. He was Clerk of Works to Henry, Prince of Wales, when Inigo Jones was his Surveyor; by 1614 Jones was Surveyor of the King's Works and Carter was Chief Clerk. Sutton directed Carter to make a survey and pressed for its completion, and he also appointed a master mason. Bricks and stone were brought to the site and early in August 1611 a dozen masons began dressing the stone.[6] Yet it seems that no construction work was carried out before Sutton's death and the alterations to the buildings were the governors' priority when they first met, in 1613. New buildings were erected to house the Brothers, the chapel was almost doubled in size, chapel cloister was erected to connect the chapel to the other buildings, and the tennis court was enlarged and adapted to house the schoolroom and the scholars' accommodation. The total cost for the establishment of the school and almshouse was just over £8000, although Sutton had assigned only £5000 for the purpose in his will.

Carter's designs were advanced, if not precocious, notably the Italianate arcades in chapel cloister and the chapel. Classical doorways, triangular pediments and decorative finials were added around the buildings. The interior was highly decorated, with colouring and gilding to the walls, woodwork and windows, notably in the principal rooms, such as the great chamber, which was further adorned by tapestries and painted glass. Whether the sense of sumptuousness would have been achieved if the parsimonious Sutton had lived to supervise the work is uncertain, but the governors clearly felt it appropriate. Among its admirers was Sir Francis Bacon, who included it in a list of buildings erected since James I's accession 'which tend to publique use and ornament'.[7]

The first of the charity's financial crises came in the early 1620s, partly as a result of the outlay on the buildings. That was overcome, as was a proposal by the Duke of Buckingham in 1624 that the Charterhouse should be closed and the endowment diverted towards the cost of creating a standing army of 10,000 or 12,000 men, to be sent to Ireland, 'or upon any other necessary service'. The plan was justified on the grounds that 'this Hospital is abused'. That Buckingham put it forward is indicative of the charity's continuing fragility, ten years after the Brothers and scholars had taken up residence. Among the arguments put forward to defeat the scheme was that to close such an institution so soon after its foundation would deter those with charitable intentions, and that it would be 'a great scandal to this State and Church, and give the Roman party just occasion to triumph'.[8]

The religious climate of Jacobean England was such that even such an issue as the nature of a charity could be interpreted in confessional terms. Yet the connections with the Carthusian priory were acknowledged, with the continued use of the name 'the Charterhouse' as a short and convenient designation for both the charity and the buildings, and the adoption of the term Poor Brothers to describe the

almsmen. It was a male-only establishment, despite the composition of the elderly population and the precedents of those almshouses that admitted both men and women. The officers were unmarried men, although the requirement was not always observed, gradually lapsed and was formally removed in 1839.

Sutton specified who should benefit only in the Letters Patent, which referred to 'poor, aged, maimed, needy and impotent people'. However, it was believed that his intention was to provide for 'distressed gentlemen', soldiers, scholars and 'men of Arte'.[9] The qualifications of the Brothers laid down by the governors were that they should be bachelors or widowers over fifty years old (but if they were maimed they could enter at forty), who had been servants to the king 'either decrepit or old Captaynes either at Sea or Land', maimed or disabled soldiers, merchants fallen on hard times, those ruined by shipwreck, fire or other calamity, or held prisoner by the Turks. Statutes promulgated in 1627 included the phrase 'gentlemen by descent and in poverty', the definition of poverty being generously set at an income of no more than £24 per annum or an estate worth less than £200.[10] Sutton's hospital did indeed provide for men who had seen 'better days', rather than those who had endured long-term poverty. The scholars were to be more than nine years old, but not over fourteen, and the sons of poor parents.[11] Each governor was entitled to nominate one candidate as a Brother or scholar when a waiting list was compiled. It also became customary for two candidates for admission to be nominated on behalf of the king, and one each in the names of the consort and the heir to the throne.

The nature of the community was maintained in subsequent regulatory instruments. In 1872 new regulations defined the beneficiaries as those who had been officers in the army or navy, clergymen, merchants, or those engaged in trading, professional, agricultural or similar occupations. They had to have come into reduced circumstances by misfortune or accident, and not by their own 'wilful default'. In the late twentieth century the category of those 'engaged in public service' was added.[12] In 1919 the prefix 'Poor' was formally dropped from the designation 'Poor Brothers' and the almsmen have since been known simply as 'the Brothers'.

After the financial problems of the early 1620s the charity was put on a sound footing during the Mastership of Sir Robert Dallington, between 1624 and 1638. It was recognised as England's foremost charity, but the close association with the church and political establishments that the founder had put in place was to expose it to hostile attention during the coming decade. The Archbishop of Canterbury served as chairman of the governors, but when the country descended into Civil War Archbishop Laud was imprisoned and some of the governors left London to join the king at Oxford. As well as its connections with the court, the charity attracted attention from Parliament's adherents because of its supposed religious leanings, evidenced by an organ and sculpted figures of Moses and Aaron and the twelve Apostles in the chapel. In 1643 Daniel Touteville, the Preacher, was sequestered by the Parliamentarian authorities.

During the Civil War the charity was affected through loss of rents from some of the country estates. The financial reserves provided a cushion during the early years of the war and thereafter expedients were employed to limit the impact on the Brothers and scholars, including some economies in the diet. The financial problems were exacerbated by the theft of roughly £1000 from the Receiver in 1650. Perhaps the greatest disruption was caused by changes in personnel, not only at the supervisory level of the governors, but among the officers, seven of whom left, absconded, were expelled or died, contributing to a period of disorganisation in the supervision of the finances and the community. On the other hand, George Garrard continued as Master throughout the 1640s and provided the stability that was needed. Parliament saw the Charterhouse not only as a possible focus for royalism but also as a

Fig 53: Communion Cup, given to the chapel in 1630 by John Postern, the first chapel clerk.

Unknown London maker.

potential resource, for the categories of those who should benefit from Sutton's charity could be interpreted as allowing places to be allocated to Parliamentarian soldiers. By 1652 the Brothers included thirty-one disabled soldiers, twenty of them officers, and some of the scholars were the sons of soldiers killed in Parliament's service.

In 1650 a report to Parliament on the charity was followed by an overhaul of its administration, with Garrard replaced as Master by Edward Cresset, and a new Preacher, George Griffith, was appointed. Under their supervision the finances were restored, as was the charity's reputation. By the late 1650s the Charterhouse had lost its earlier identity as a royalist stronghold and Oliver Cromwell's widow, Elizabeth, and their daughter Frances, widow of Robert Rich, took refuge there as the republican regime collapsed in 1660 and the monarchy was restored. But the extent to which the charity was embedded within the political and religious system was emphasised by the speed with which the changes made over the previous ten years were then reversed. As a Baptist, Cresset could not continue in his post, although it was acknowledged that he 'deserved in many respects very well of that house and therefore Received publicke thankes from the Lords the Governors 1660 upon his dismission out of it'. Griffith was displaced in July 1661; five Brothers who refused to attend services and take the sacrament were expelled.[13]

The charity was fortunate during the calamities that struck London in the mid-1660s, with 'hardly a head aking of above 40 left in the house in the great sicknesse year 1665 and not a tenement belonging to it touched in the fire time 1666'.[14] But a fire in 1671 destroyed a part of the Brothers' lodgings. The replacement building was designed by Sir Christopher Wren. The charity's prosperity became increasingly fragile in the late seventeenth century, as prices for both arable produce and livestock fell. Tenants asked for their debts to be cancelled or their rents reduced, the annual account showed a deficit in some years and rent arrears grew steadily. The doubtful ability and questionable honesty of some of the staff undoubtedly contributed to the charity's problems. Most seriously, during the period when William Lightfoot was Registrar (1674–99), Robert Payne was Receiver (1676–1717) and Richard Spour was Auditor (1670–1717), the three men connived to defraud the charity of a sum probably equivalent to two years' revenue. There had been earlier problems with the financial officers, but nothing on that scale had been discovered.

The financial corruption occurred during a period when the charity was closely connected to London's intellectual community. Among the Masters were Martin Clifford and Thomas Burnet, two of the most distinguished men to hold the post. Clifford was the second Duke of Buckingham's secretary and a writer who attracted attention as a prominent literary critic of John Dryden. His major work was *A Treatise of Humane Reason* (1675), which cogently argues the case for religious toleration. While Clifford was Master, the first published history of the charity appeared, in 1677, as *Domus Carthusiana; or, an Account ... of the Charter-House near Smithfield in London*. The author, Samuel Herne, based his account partly upon an anonymous manuscript compiled in 1669 and it is a commendatory account, containing the inaccurate observation that 'the Revenues are no way embezel'd'.[15] Burnet, who was appointed in May 1685, was a clergyman whose abilities were such that he was considered a possible future Archbishop of Canterbury. He published, in 1681, the first two books of his major work, *Telluris theoria sacra*, translated at Charles II's request, and reissued as *Sacred Theory of the Earth*. The two final books appeared in 1689 and by 1726 the work had gone through six editions. His *Archaeologiae Philosophicae: sive Doctrina antiqua de rerum originibus* appeared in 1692, dedicated to William III. Burnet's allegorical treatment of scripture and the thesis that God had created the world through natural causes, not miracles, were too controversial to gain acceptance by the church and he was not appointed to any senior post.

Fig 54: Benjamin Laney, Bishop of Ely, c.1670, two years after he had been made a governor.

Oil painting, attributed to Peter Lely (1618–1680).

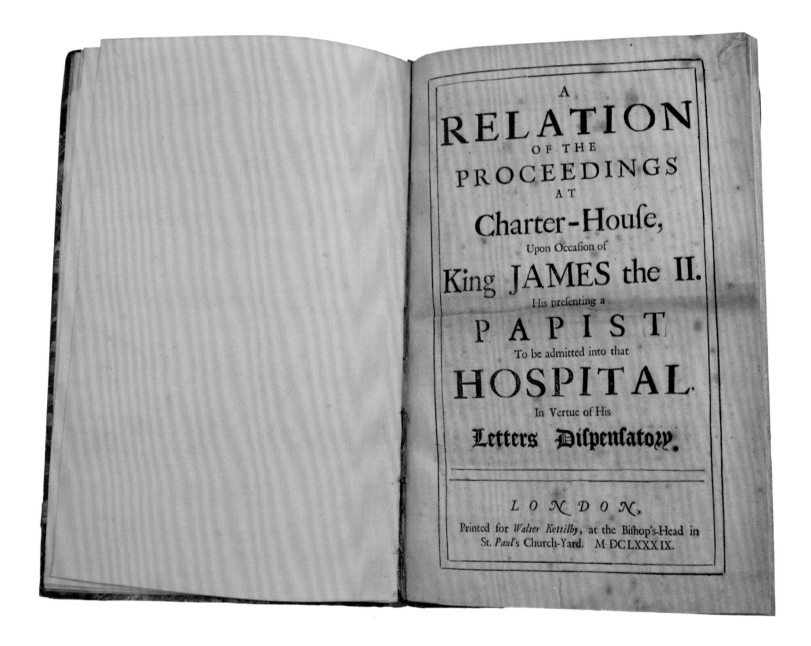

A
RELATION
OF THE
PROCEEDINGS
AT
Charter-House,
Upon Occasion of
King JAMES the II.
His presenting a
PAPIST
To be admitted into that
HOSPITAL.
In Vertue of His
Letters Dispensatory.

LONDON,
Printed for _Walter Kettilby_, at the Bishop's-Head in
St. _Paul's_ Church-Yard. M DC LXXXIX.

Fig 55: The title page of Thomas Burnet's defence of
his actions in defying King James II's wish to admit a
Catholic as a Brother, 1689.

Early in Burnet's period as Master the charity clashed with the court over James II's attempt to use his supposed dispensing power and appoint a Roman Catholic as a Brother. Candidates had to take the Oaths of Allegiance and Supremacy before they could enter, but the king sent Andrew Popham with a letter to the governors, directing that they should admit him without him being required to take the oaths. Burnet intervened and ruled that the governors should discuss the matter before Popham could be admitted, and when they did so, in January 1687, he pointed out that the Act of Parliament of 1628 required that all governors, officers and Brothers had to take the oaths prior to admission. When a governor questioned whether this was relevant, Burnet was supported by the Duke of Ormond, who commented that 'an Act of Parliament was not so slight a thing, but that it deserv'd to be consider'd'. After some discussion, the motion that Popham should be admitted was defeated and George Jeffreys and some other governors who supported the court angrily left the meeting. A later attempt to revive the issue was equally unsuccessful. This was seen as the first of the steps to oppose the king's attempt to introduce Roman Catholics into public offices. In 1689, after the Glorious Revolution had displaced James, Burnet published, anonymously, his account of the controversy as *A Relation of the Proceedings at Charter-House, upon Occasion of King James the II. His presenting a Papist to be admitted into that Hospital*.[16] The almshouse was highly regarded, especially among Whig writers. In 1691 Guy Miège described the charity as 'This noble Foundation not to be parallelled by any Subject in Europe', and in the 1720s Daniel Defoe gave it generous praise indeed as 'the greatest and noblest gift that ever was given for charity, by any one man, public or private, in this nation, since history gives us any account of things'.[17]

The eighteenth century was a much calmer period for the Charterhouse. John King, the Preacher, succeeded Burnet in 1715 and under his direction the finances had recovered so well that in 1726 the expensive task of renovating the chapel was undertaken. King's successor, Nicholas Mann, was followed by Philip Bearcroft, who published in 1737 another history, entitled *An Historical Account of Thomas Sutton Esq: and of his Foundation in Charter-House*, in which he pointed out that Charterhouse had the unique distinction among charities, schools and colleges to be 'governed always by the Chief Personages of the State'. They included Sir Robert Walpole, the first Prime Minister, who took an active interest in the nominations for Brothers. Those places were a source of patronage and before the end of the seventeenth century it was alleged that the governors nominated their own former servants as pensioners, both to reward their services and to avoid the expense of maintaining them when they were old. That claim was to surface intermittently until the mid-nineteenth century.

With the right of nomination and attendance at the governors' assemblies went membership of the standing committee and dealing with matters that may broadly be termed 'pastoral'. In 1734 the 'rude and disorderly behaviour of some Pensioners' complained of by the Master was referred to the Bishop of London, Edmund Gibson. Just three years later he was trying to deal with John Vince, a Brother alleged to have used 'many profane Oaths and Curses' when speaking to the Master and refusing to 'dismiss a Woman that had kept him company for several years in his Chamber night & day'. Clearly a difficult man, Vince failed to turn up for his meeting with the bishop. A later Bishop of London, Beilby Porteous, was also drawn into the petty jealousies within the community when he received from an anonymous Brother a vituperatively critical summary of the state of the almshouse, which spared no one. Even the Manciple, cook, butler and gardener were damned for their 'Rapacity & plunder', and the butler was criticised for selling some of the beer supplies, which were better than those that he was serving to the Brothers.[18] The quality of the food and drink, and the prices paid for them, were long-term

Fig 56: Plaster overmantel with the figures of Faith, Hope and Charity, installed in the Master's rooms around 1625.

concerns for the Brothers and two of them routinely went to the market with the Manciple, as a check on his purchases.

In the early eighteenth century food and drink accounted for more than a third of the charity's expenditure and was the largest category in the budget. But as agricultural prices rose in the late eighteenth century and the early nineteenth so did rents and the charity was able to accumulate a financial surplus. Some of this was spent on new accommodation for the Brothers, the majority of whom still lived in the buildings erected in 1614 and the Wren Building. The Brothers' rooms in the buildings around Master's Court had steadily been reallocated, chiefly as additions to the officers' quarters, as they were allowed to marry and live with their families in the hospital, and to use their space for their private practice. The Physician's house at the gate had been rebuilt in 1716 and by the end of the eighteenth century the Organist's apartment consisted of a sitting room, a library and five bedrooms. The greatest expansion was that of the Master's Lodge, originally five rooms on the first floor of the east wing of Master's Court, but expanded on to both floors and also incorporating the former long gallery in the south range and the buildings on the south side of Chapel Court. In the 1840s the range between Chapel Court and the square was rebuilt and the lodge then contained thirty-three rooms.

The Wren Building and the adjoining residential ranges were demolished in the mid-1820s and replaced by new accommodation that cost £46,319, equivalent to more than two years' revenue. This was the most expensive building programme since the conversion of the mansion in 1613–14 and replaced the former layout with two rectangular courts. The new arrangement respected the Brothers' burial ground, which was left undisturbed in the open space of Pensioners' Court, although it was no longer used and a new one was consecrated beyond the north side of the court. Further work followed, with additions to Preacher's Court in 1839–41, designed by Edward Blore. The new ranges

in the two courts provided rooms for the Brothers, paired on either side of staircases, an apartment for the Preacher in the north-east corner of Preacher's Court and a house for the Manciple on its east side. Between the two quads was an arcaded ground storey, which, with the crenellated buildings in a 'Tudor' style, created an atmosphere reminiscent of an Oxbridge college. Blore also remodelled the chapel, taking down the organ gallery in the south aisle and moving its decorative front to the gallery at the end of the north aisle. That gallery was adapted for a new organ, installed in 1842. The governors and officers were displaced from that gallery and given new pews in the upper gallery of an addition built in 1824 when the number of pupils was especially high, which had proved to be a short-lived phase.

Other reforms made in the same period included new arrangements for the Brothers' care and the women who had cleaned the Brothers' rooms were replaced by ten nurses. In 1829 an infirmary was provided in Preacher's Court for the Brothers and also a consulting room and a dispensary, where the Physician, now the Medical Officer, could dispense medicines, without having to pay an apothecary for every dose. The Medical Officer's duties included regular reports on the health of the Brothers and scholars.

Another change was made in 1832, when the staff's perquisites in kind, such as taking food left over at the end of a meal and unwanted clothes, were abolished and their salaries were raised to compensate them. The previous arrangement at mealtimes had been that each man helped himself from the dish in turn, with his own knife. Bread had been issued not with the meat, but after dinner, and so those Brothers who preferred to take bread with their meat were obliged to keep some from the previous day, and they also had to collect beer from the buttery before the meal, carry it to their rooms and then into the hall. On some days the Brothers took butter or a piece of pie or pudding to their rooms at the end of the meal. With the new arrangements those practices were

Fig 57: The 'grace paddle', decorated with Thomas Sutton's arms: the other side has a short prayer read aloud by the Master before lunch.

Photograph by Tom Hobson

ended and the Brothers were served food individually, not in mess groups of five, and could eat and drink as much as they required, as the servants no longer needed the food that was left over. This was designed to bring more orderliness and decorum to mealtimes. The Master's table was moved to Brooke Hall, mainly so that he and his guests could follow polite society in dining later. Space then became available in the great hall for all of the Brothers and from 1846 the upper hall was the scholars' dining-hall, approached from the school along the Norfolk Cloister.

The reforms were overseen by William Hale, who had been a pupil at the school and had returned to the charity as Preacher in 1823; he was appointed Master in 1842 and held the post until his death in 1870. He was the dominant figure in the charity over the mid-nineteenth century period and, although a pluralist and outwardly a conservative figure, he achieved considerable change at the Charterhouse.

Despite the improvements, the charity was fiercely attacked in 1852 in an article in Charles Dickens's popular and influential periodical *Household Words*, which had a circulation of 38,000 and a much wider readership, as copies were handed around. It contrasted the officers' stipends and the scale of their apartments with the Brothers' accommodation and pensions. Their living conditions and the rules imposed upon them were not appropriate for men in their position, and they feared being chastised. Hale was singled out as 'the great pluralist' who occupied a 'luxuriously fitted' apartment, and for those who held a senior post in the charity the Brothers were regarded as 'simply the discomforts of the place; which otherwise provides good salaries, and dwellings, and dinners, and daily pints of wine to the gentlemen and ladies who are really fed upon its funds'. Hale wrote a cogent response outlining the improvements that had been made and the problems that were faced by the officers and staff, such as drunkenness. It was privately published by the governors as a pamphlet and so made little impact compared to the piece in *Household Words*, which carried a second

article in 1855 along the lines of the first attack.[19] The Brothers' reaction was to ask for an increase in their pensions, which was granted.

The articles asked who should benefit from a place in the almshouse and who actually was living there as a Brother. Hale grouped the Brothers broadly into the categories of tradesmen, clerks and servants. They included fifteen military and naval men, eight merchants, seven schoolmasters and literary men, and five had practised law or medicine. Those admitted during the preceding ten years had also included booksellers, stationers, innkeepers, farmers, coal merchants, a clock- and watchmaker, a sugar refiner, a silversmith, a florist and an organ builder, suggesting a range of backgrounds not readily classifiable into social categories.

A more effective response than Hale's came from the novelist William Makepeace Thackeray, who had also been a pupil at the school, where he had been most unhappy, according to his own account. In his novel *The Newcomes*, written between 1853 and 1855, he presented a picture of the Charterhouse that was sympathetic, if overly sentimental and rather idealised. His character Thomas Newcome was one of the Brothers, having gone bankrupt. He was a retired soldier who had lost his money through no fault of his own, and he had scrupulously repaid those from whom he had borrowed. His very proper conduct showed him to be a true gentleman and Thackeray makes the reader aware of both the shame felt by a bankrupt and the humiliation for someone from a respectable background being forced by his circumstances to spend his final years in an almshouse. But his conditions were good, his room was 'neat and comfortable' and he was treated respectfully by the staff. Thackeray's account was so influential that it helped to establish a positive image of the Charterhouse that was to endure well into the twentieth century.

Thackeray spoke at the annual Founder's Day dinner in 1863, held on 12 December, and died on Christmas Eve. He sat opposite William

Haig Brown, newly appointed as Headmaster, the first non-Carthusian to hold the post since 1626. The proposal to separate the school from the almshouse had been discussed intermittently for some years, and Haig Brown became an effective advocate of separation, which was achieved by the Public Schools Act of 1868. Hale had opposed the change, but acquiesced with good grace. The title of 'The Hospital of King James founded in Charterhouse' was dropped and the almshouse was named 'Sutton's Hospital in Charterhouse'. In the summer of 1872 the school moved into its new buildings at Godalming. Much of the cost of the site and the buildings was paid for by the sale of the eastern part of the Charterhouse site to the Merchant Taylors' Company, for its school. The company demolished the old school building and the adjoining section of the Norfolk Cloister. The remainder of the cloister was not included in the sale. With the scholars gone, the upper hall was not needed for a dining room and became the Brothers' library.

Other changes followed, for within a few years of the division of the charity the agricultural depression of the late nineteenth century set in and falling prices of farm produce led to a steep decline in rental income. The charity could no longer maintain the full complement of Brothers and in 1882 the number was reduced to sixty-eight and from 1915 it was reduced further, to fifty, before an improvement in revenues allowed an increase, to sixty-one in 1931 and sixty-three by 1939. With its diminished income the charity could do no more than maintain the buildings, which became progressively shabbier. The decline was such that the governors considered selling the site of the almshouse itself for a housing development and paying the Brothers out-pensions for them to live in lodging houses. A Bill was introduced in the House of Lords in 1886 and it passed, but it met such opposition in the Commons that it was withdrawn before the vote was taken. One of the governors, who spoke in the Commons, commented that 'the beautiful and romantic picture' of the Charterhouse conveyed by Thackeray had contributed to the interest in the Bill, reflected in the number of Members who were in the chamber to hear the debate, and the extent of the opposition. [20]

Among the changes that followed the departure of the school was the admissions process. The Charity Commissioners' Scheme of 1872 raised the admission age to sixty and would-be Brothers now applied directly to the almshouse and were interviewed by the Master. Those admitted were then assigned to a governor. The Archbishop of Canterbury continued to act as chairman of the governors, it had become customary for the Archbishop of York to be a governor, and nineteen of the twenty Prime Ministers during the century served in the role, the sole exception being the Earl of Rosebery. In contrast, the only Prime Minister to serve during the twentieth century was Stanley Baldwin.

The low levels of rents continued into the early twentieth century and so the decision was taken to sell the country estates, most of which were bequeathed by Sutton or bought by the governors with his legacy. That was mostly carried through in 1919; the revival of agricultural prosperity during the First World War had revitalised the market in rural land and made it an opportune time to sell. The proceeds were invested in securities, which provided a more stable and predictable income than the landed estates and were easier and cheaper to administer. With the continued low level of receipts, even after the sale of the country estates, the financial problems remained and by the beginning of the Second World War the Master was preparing to implement some severe economies. But his plans were thwarted by enemy action.

The London County Council initiated a programme of precautions against the impact of aerial bombardments, which it carried through in 1939. They included the sinking of water tanks in Charterhouse Square and the placing of others on the pavement along the boundary wall adjoining the gatehouse. Within the Charterhouse, air-raid shelters were constructed in Preacher's Court and a large shelter in the garden between Pensioners' Court and Clerkenwell Road, for

Fig 58: **The chimneypiece in the great hall.**

Photograph by Tom Hobson

public use. The governors considered evacuating the Brothers, but that would have required leasing or buying adequate premises out of London and hiring fire-watchers to spot the fall of firebombs, to protect the historic buildings: and so the Brothers remained at the Charterhouse and acted as fire-watchers. All went well for much of the Blitz, until the last big raid, on the night of 10–11 May 1941, which caused extensive damage in the City. A firebomb went unnoticed and started a blaze in the roof of the range next to the chapel. Driven by a north-easterly wind, the flames spread southwards and westwards, gutting the ranges around Master's Court, much of Wash-house Court, the kitchens, the Registrar's house, the great hall, great staircase, great chamber and the library, but the chapel was undamaged. There were no casualties, and because of the long interval between the first alarm and the fire running out of control many movable objects were rescued in advance of the flames. The accommodation in Pensioners' and Preacher's Courts was not affected, but without the service areas the buildings were no longer usable and were evacuated. Two former nursing homes in Godalming were acquired for the Brothers' accommodation.

The architect Sir Charles Peers was one of the governors and he prepared a report on the strategy for rebuilding. On his recommendation the partnership of the Hon. John Seely (from 1947 Lord Mottistone) and Paul Paget were appointed as architects. They had remodelled the old chapel at Charterhouse School as a music school in 1940 and they had the further advantage that their offices were close by, in Cloth Fair. Their designs were first presented to the governors in May 1944 and were favourably received, but the long-term future of the site depended on the War Damage Commission's contribution to the reinstatement of the damaged buildings; it was unable to finance rebuilding to a new plan, or on another site.

Although Seely & Paget's proposals were accepted and the Commission's approval was obtained, there were long delays before the work could begin and progress was slow even when it was underway. The licensing system for key materials, operated by the Ministry of Works, was not abolished until 1954 and Britain's participation in the Korean War from 1950 to 1953 created difficulties with the supply of materials required by the armaments industry. The situation was not helped by the relatively low priority afforded to an almshouse, compared with industrial buildings and housing. Licences were issued by the Ministry for only relatively small sections of work at a time, imposing a piecemeal approach to the restoration. Paget later recalled that the industry had been 'ham-strung with acute shortage of material on the one hand and the extreme restrictions imposed by the Building Licensing system on the other'.[21] The restoration began in 1949 and continued until 1957.

The Brothers' accommodation was moved from Pensioners' and Preacher's Courts into Wash-house Court and the rebuilt ranges around Master's Court. Fewer Brothers were to be cared for than before the war, because of the level of the charity's income available for their maintenance, and so all of the residential and catering rooms could be placed within the block formed by the Tudor and Jacobean buildings. This had the advantage that all of the Brothers could reach the communal rooms under cover. Their rooms occupied the space of the former Master's Lodge, with the Medical Officer moved to a flat in Preacher's Court and his house assigned to the Master. That part of the former lodge on the south side of Chapel Court was not rebuilt and the Blore ranges in Preacher's Court were demolished, while the Brothers' rooms in Pensioners' Court were let to private tenants. The principal rooms were restored, but not the great staircase, which was replaced by a new staircase in a different position. Externally, the layer of render was removed, as was the brick skin added to the ranges fronting Master's Court in the mid-eighteenth century. As an economy, the turret on the roof of the great hall was not rebuilt. Removal of the crenellation from

Fig 59: **The door between the Chapel and Chapel Cloister, badly burnt in May 1941.**

Photograph by Lawrence Watson

Fig 60: *The Old Charterhouse*, lithograph by Edward
Ardizzone, 1964.

Courtesy Estate of Edward Ardizzone

the Pensioners' Court buildings gave them a plainer appearance.

No new Brothers were admitted after the evacuation and the number had fallen to thirteen by 1951, the year in which they returned. At first new rooms around Wash-house Court were occupied, while the remainder of the buildings were repaired. When that work was completed the number of Brothers was increased, to thirty-two, with three further rooms for infirmary cases. Praised as a 'most skilful and successful reconstruction', Seely & Paget's work produced the modern Charterhouse buildings.

The space left by the demolished buildings on the east side of Preacher's Court was incorporated into a garden and another garden was created above the remains of the building on the west side. In the late 1970s and early 1980s only twenty-seven Brothers were in residence, but with an improvement in the charity's finances it became possible to erect new buildings with rooms for the Brothers. They replaced the demolished buildings on the west side of Preacher's Court and were built to the designs of Michael Hopkins & Partners. Completed in 2000 and designated the Admiral Ashmore Building, they finally concluded the post-war restoration. The range between Preacher's and Pensioners' Courts was then converted into an infirmary. Those improvements were followed by the renovation of the Brothers' rooms in the historic core and by 2015 there was accommodation for forty-five Brothers.

The restored buildings provided a modern home for the Brothers and there were other changes. Because old-age pensions were providing a sufficient income, from 1956 the Brothers' pensions were phased out and from 1984 they contributed to the cost of their accommodation. The wearing of gowns was no longer required, nor was attendance at chapel compulsory.

From its beginnings in the reign of James I, Sutton's Hospital has provided for successive generations of pensioners. The enforced absence of the Brothers between 1941 and 1951 has been the only break in the charity's use of the site as an almshouse. It occupies a group of buildings that was built in the mid-sixteenth century as an aristocratic mansion and incorporates parts of the Carthusian priory founded in 1371 on a Black Death burial ground of 1349. Through changing times the governors and officers have maintained the charity's fundamental purpose and it has continued as the beneficiary of Thomas Sutton's fortune and his enduring legacy.

References

1 Hugh Trevor-Roper, 'Thomas Sutton (1532–1611)', *Oxford Dictionary of National Biography* (Oxford, 2004).

2 Neal R. Shipley, 'Thomas Sutton: Tudor-Stuart Moneylender', *Business History Review*, I/4 (1976), 461, 466–8.

3 Neal R. Shipley, '"Full Hand and Worthy Purposes": the Foundation of Charterhouse, 1610–1616', *Guildhall Studies in London History*, I/4 (1975), 229–49.

4 London Metropolitan Archives, acc/1876/G/1/1/1.

5 Shipley, '"Full Hand and Worthy Purposes"', 241; London Metropolitan Archives, acc/1876/F/9/1; Oxford, Bodleian Library, MS Tanner 161, fol. 8.

6 London Metropolitan Archives, acc/1876/F/3/5/50-52, 56; /F/9/31; /F/9/48/14th bk.

7 James F. Larkin and Paul L. Hughes, eds, *Stuart Royal Proclamations*, I: *Royal Proclamations of King James I, 1603–1625* (Oxford, 1973), 346.

8 Stephen Porter, *The London Charterhouse: A History of Thomas Sutton's Charity* (Stroud, 2009), 22–3.

9 London Metropolitan Archives, acc/1876/F/3/1,3.

10 *Charter, Acts of Parliament, and Governors' Statutes for the Foundation and Government of the Charterhouse* (London, 1832), 50.

11 Charterhouse Muniments [CM], G/2/1, 3, 18.

12 Gerald S. Davies, *Charterhouse in London: Monastery, Mansion, Hospital, School* (London, 1921), 231; CM, Brothers' Regulations, 1908, 1928; Statutory Instruments, 1983 No.588, The Charities (Sutton's Hospital in Charterhouse) Order 1983, 7.

13 Porter, *London Charterhouse*, 31–43, 48–9.

14 British Library, Lansdowne MS 1198, fol. 23.

15 Samuel Herne, *Domus Carthusiana, or, an account of the Most Noble Foundation of the Charter-House … with the life … of Thomas Sutton, esq., the founder thereof …* (London, 1677), 197.

16 Porter, *London Charterhouse*, 60–62.

17 Guy Miege, *The New State of England Under Their Majesties K. William and Q. Mary* (London, 1691), 302; Daniel Defoe, *A Tour through the Whole Island of Great Britain*, ed. Pat Rogers (Harmondsworth, 1971), 334.

18 CM, G/2/4, 5 passim; London, Lambeth Palace Library, Beilby Porteous papers, vol. 3, fols 131–2.

19 [William Thomas Moncrieff and Henry Morley], 'The Poor Brothers of the Charterhouse', *Household Words*, V, no. 116 (12 June 1852), 288–91; [Henry Morley], 'Charter-House Charity', *Household Words*, XII, no. 297 (1 Dec. 1855), 409–14; [William Hale Hale], *Some Account of the Early History and Foundation of the Hospital of King James, Founded in Charterhouse* (London, 1854).

20 Hansard, *Commons Debates*, vol. 305, 3rd ser., 7 May 1886, col. 503.

21 Letter to Whinney, 13 July 1971, Royal Institute of British Architects, Seely & Paget Archive, box 34.

Fig 61: **The 'grace paddle', with the bell and gavel used every day before lunch at the Charterhouse.**

Photograph by Lawrence Watson

A Boy's-eye View of Charterhouse School

Catherine Smith

The organisation and running of the School ('Charterhouse') at its London site is well documented in the Assembly order books, which minute every meeting of the governing body from 1613 onwards. However, the everyday life of pupils at Charterhouse is less well recorded, as even the names of many of the earlier pupils are unknown. This chapter will seek to bring to life the experience of a nineteenth-century boy at Charterhouse by focusing on original sources, such as pupils' letters, reminiscences and diaries.

Charterhouse School provided the traditional classical education that was essential in order to go to university and it also offered good opportunities to gain apprenticeships for those boys seeking a secure future in a trade or craft. By the nineteenth century few boys were taking up formal apprenticeships, but many still went straight into family businesses or gained commissions into the Army. Thomas Sutton's foundation offered free scholarships for up to forty (later increased to sixty) 'poore scholars', each nominated by a member of the governing body. Although any prospective scholar was required to be 'well entred in learning answerable to his age', it was also crucial for his parents to be well connected in order to gain the patronage of a governor. Scholars (known as 'Gownboys' because of their distinctive dress) had to be at least nine years old and no more than fourteen when they took up their scholarship. Poverty was a relative term in this context and included any family that did not have property for their children to inherit, so many scholars were the sons of middle-class professionals.[1] Scholars not only received a free classical education, but food, accommodation and clothing, plus funding towards either a university education or a trade apprenticeship. It was not until the school moved to Godalming in 1872 that governors' nominations were abolished and scholarships were awarded solely on the basis of academic ability.

The first Schoolmaster's salary was originally set at £20 per annum (increased to £240 by 1862) and the Usher (assistant master) received £10 per annum (£140 in 1862): but it was always assumed that they could augment their salaries by taking fee-paying pupils, either as day boys or as private boarders; the Schoolmaster could also use these fees to employ extra assistant masters when needed. The governors only required accounts for pupils receiving free scholarships, so no records were kept of the early fee-paying pupils and most are completely unknown. It is thought that there were generally about sixty day boys attending the School, although the numbers varied. Masters often had private boarders lodging with them, though this too was not fully recorded until 1795 when the governors introduced an annual return of boarders in all the boarding houses.

CLOTHES

Gownboy scholars wore short black academic gowns (hence their name) over a short dark-coloured jerkin or jacket and knee breeches, and mortar boards. The governors' order book specifies that the school tailor should also provide the scholars with shoes (known as Gowsers), stockings, garters (to hold up the stockings), a hat and hat band, girdles and points (laces used before buttons became more prevalent) and gloves; scholars were also issued with three shirts a year, with eight bands (collars), plus a supply of books, paper, ink and quill pens.[2] This uniform changed little in more than two and a half centuries, apart from the replacement of breeches with trousers sometime in the mid-nineteenth century and the introduction of caps instead of hats in 1805.

Fee-paying pupils were not required to wear a uniform. Printed bills for Mr Churton's private boarders in 1823 specified that boys should bring with them eight shirts, six pairs of worsted stockings, eight pairs of cotton stockings, six pocket handkerchiefs, three nightshirts, three nightcaps, six towels and combs and brushes. Extra costs for purchases from the school tailor, shoemaker, hair-cutter, apothecary and bookseller could be added to the termly bill as required. The tailor had

---

Fig 62: **A Gownboy in his regulation uniform, as worn around 1870.**

Photograph courtesy Charterhouse School Archives

Fig 63: **Page from the Epicure Club's Minute Book: recording a concert performance in Gownboys Hall, 24 November 1864.**

Photograph courtesy Charterhouse School Archives

Fig 64: **The sixth form, c.1870.**

Photograph courtesy Charterhouse School Archives

a workshop in an attic above the governors' state rooms, which was out of bounds unless boys were delivering clothes to be repaired or placing new orders. However, a pupil during the 1820s remembered it as a good location for clandestine parties at weekends when the tailor was off duty.[3] A drawing made by William Thackeray while at Charterhouse in the 1820s shows a fellow pupil wearing a rather tattered, but fashionable, pale blue jacket with a fancy collar and patched white trousers.

Then as now, wearing the right fashion mattered to teenagers, causing Alfred Saunders to complain not long after his arrival at school in 1867, 'tell Sarah that I am using my best coat every day because the other has a button as large as a saucer and I can't possibly wear it'. Alfred wrote to his sister, Aggy, in 1870, 'I ordered a light blue tie because of the Boat Race. Nearly all the fellows are getting them and I decidedly prefer Cambridge at present.' Additional clothes could be made and the cost added to the end of term bill: Saunders wrote home, 'Please write by return of post and tell me I may have a new flannel shirt. I have worn my last nearly every day for the last year and a half and it is dreadfully ragged. It will only cost about 8 shillings.' Anticipating his mother's reaction, he added, 'PS when I say I have worn my shirt every day I don't quite mean that you know because of course it has been to the wash dozens of times and that *wears* it out dreadfully.'

FOOD

Food features frequently in schoolboy letters from the Charterhouse. The basic rations in the early years of the school sound very austere to us, but it should be remembered that food was far less plentiful and varied for the population as a whole and the variety and quantity of food available in the twenty-first century would have been unimaginable. The scholars were woken at 5:00am and had two hours of early school before stopping for breakfast at 8:00am, consisting of bread, cheese and beer.[4] Water supplies were unreliable and waterborne diseases such as cholera

and dysentery were an ever-present threat, so weak 'small beer' was a safer option for both adults and children; as late as 1900 beer was still being offered to the pupils with meals.[5]

Dinner was the main meal, eaten at some point between midday and 3:00pm, including beef, mutton, pork or veal, with fish on Fridays. John Wesley complained that for his first four years at Charterhouse he survived on dry bread, and not much of that, because the older boys stole his meat. Supper at 7:00pm consisted of yet more bread, cheese and beer. Boys who were hungry between meals could ask for a snack, known as a 'beevor', of bread and milk at the Buttery. The governors' weekly order book suggests that there was actually a little more variety in the boys' diet, as it lists a range of food, including furmity (porridge) and apple pies. William MacPherson, writing in 1824 as a twelve-year-old new boy, also records a slightly better diet: 'we have hot rolls and butter and milk and water to breakfast (tea 3 times a week). We have roast to dinner, soup and plum pudding twice a week and hot milk and plain bread to supper.' However, there is no mention of fresh fruit or vegetables.

A set of rules for day boys, printed in the 1820s, states that 'the bringing in of provisions etc for boarders is strictly forbidden', suggesting that the boarders craved more variety and quantity in their diet. Alfred Saunders wrote regularly to his sister Aggy between 1867 and 1871, often including pleas for cheese, jam, cakes, biscuits, plum pudding, figs and oranges. There was a small tuck shop, open for just two hours twice a week, in a basement room under the schoolroom and this sold a limited range of 'catpies', sausage rolls, fruit tarts, bathbuns, penny buns and abernethies.[6]

ACCOMMODATION

The Gownboy scholars were housed in a building that had started life as the Duke of Norfolk's indoor tennis court. In 1614 it was converted into a dining hall and common room (the 'writing school') with several dormitories upstairs. By the eighteenth century the building had fallen into serious disrepair, the dormitory windows had been blocked up and the only light and ventilation came from holes in the walls.[7] Major repairs were undertaken in the 1760s, but 'Gownboys' was never a palatial residence. The dormitories were divided up into cubicles, each with one bed shared by two boys and it was not until 1805 that pupils were all provided with individual beds; school bills for the period proudly state that 'a single bed is included in the annual charge', as though this was a significant bonus.[8] At night the Gownboys were locked into their building to prevent them from roaming freely – a dangerous practice, considering the risk of fire. If somebody was ill or anything was needed during the night the boys would bang on the walls with their boots until the Housemaster came to see what the problem was.[9] This lack of supervision was not at all unusual in schools, as the only responsibility of a teacher was to convey knowledge to his charges in whatever way was most effective, without any expectation that he should offer pastoral care or any supervision outside the classroom.

Private boarding houses had similar arrangements, with often overcrowded dormitories and sparse facilities. Henry Liddell described the Long Room of Watkinson's boarding house as:

> a low, dark, dirty apartment … Here we breakfasted, dined and supped; and this was our only sitting room. The upper boys had cupboards between the windows and a sort of table-desk in front of each cupboard, so that the doors of the cupboards being open they formed a sort of screen, and enabled them to read and write in comparative privacy. The lower boys sat on benches placed along the dining tables, and while the upper boys were at work were compelled, on pain of prompt punishment, to keep absolute silence … Each boy had a small locker of two shelves, in which he kept his books and whatever else he chose.'[10]

Boys were also encouraged to read for pleasure and each boarding house had its own library of popular literature, poetry, non-fiction and newspapers, selected by a Library Committee. Other unofficial evening pastimes included carving names into the furniture (an activity known as 'mobbing'); several examples of 'mobbed' desks have survived in the school's museum collection (Fig. 66).

SICKNESS

Boys' minor ailments were treated by their House Matron and those with infectious illnesses were isolated in the Infirmary. The School Medical Officer visited the boarding houses each morning to examine any patients and administer treatment for minor ailments. Gerald Davies described the Medical Officer as 'a man whose knowledge of human nature perhaps was in advance of his medical science' and who used the same two panaceas for all his patients: a 'black draught' of unknown content for those who might be faking illness and a 'brown draught' for those who seemed genuinely unwell.[11] Fear of these unpleasant medications kept most boys away from the sickroom. For some, however, the matron's infirmary was a haven from the dreariness of school life. One enterprising teenager faked illness in order to write an elaborate illustrated Valentine letter to the girl of his dreams:

> Most exquisite and adorable Miss Polina, I am shamming ill today to escape school and to find time to write a Valentine to the fair charmer of my soul. I know you'll feel for me when you know what I am suffering this morning for your sweet sake. I have been obliged to swallow an odious black Draught, and have had nothing but a large basin of Water Gruel for my breakfast. But I don't care! My beloved Polina Lewis makes up for all! It is a comfort to me here to have something in the shape of a woman to talk to of my love for you, though that woman is only Mother J.[12]

'Mother J' was the Gownboys' Matron, Mrs Elizabeth Jeffkins, who held the post for more than thirty years and was described as 'thoughtfulness and gentleness personified'. She died at Charterhouse in 1856 and a pupil of the time recalled visiting her deathbed and 'looking upon her lying in her shell, placid, serene and wax-like, and returning to hockey as if death had been only an ordinary item in our existence'.[13] A memorial to Mrs Jeffkins, paid for by her Gownboys, was placed in the chapel. Children were not shielded from the realities of death and it would not have been considered unusual or inappropriate for quite young children to visit the deathbed of friends and relatives. In an age before penicillin and mass vaccinations, there were also inevitably some childhood deaths. When Matthew Lushington died from smallpox at Charterhouse on 24 December 1754, his Schoolmaster, Revd Dr Lewis Crusius, had the sad task of writing to his parents: 'You may be assured that no attention nor care was omitted to save the life of the dear youth. But Dr Hawis was under great apprehensions from the first appearance of his illness and this occasioned my silence, as I had no heart to be the harbinger of bad news. We are very sorry for the loss and can only pray God to comfort you.'[14]

Hygiene was primitive: the washing facilities in Gownboys consisted of 'a long, broad, shallow leaden trough, into which discharged about half a dozen common cocks [taps]. Boys were expected to wash each day, but this may not have left them much cleaner:

About ten minutes before morning school there was a great rush downstairs, the stream separated, each boy to his drawer for his tooth-brush … As each reached the front he turned the cock about half open, so as to secure only a moderate splashing, and proceeded to wash his teeth … This done, and it was a very short process, a cake of the 'house soap' that was in common use, was secured, and the hands were washed, after a fashion. Then the cock was turned nearly full on, the hands were formed into a cup, filled with water, and so the face was washed. The dripping youth then shoved his way through the crowd to the jack towel which hung on one side and there wiped off the remains of his ablutions. We were not particular, but it was desirable to gain the towel as early as possible, since only one was allowed for the whole twenty or thirty who were to be dried, and this unlucky towel was to last two days. Each boy then retreated to his drawer, brushed and combed his hair, put on his gown, took up his books and scampered off to school.[15]

In the winter the pipes froze, in which case the only water available came from large outdoor pumps. Baths were only possible if the butler and his wife heated a large cauldron of water to fill a bathtub in front of the kitchen fire. E. P. Eardley-Wilmot recalled that the butler's wife supervised the bath time of the youngest boys on Friday afternoons after school, providing a welcome sanctuary and comforting supper treats at the same time.[16]

NEW BOYS AND THE FAGGING SYSTEM

Arrival at Charterhouse must have been a daunting experience. New boys were sent straight to the School Medical Officer for a health check, then to the Schoolmaster to assess which form they should be placed in, and then to meet their fellow pupils, who would greet them with a barrage of questions, always starting with 'What's your name? Who's your father? And how much money have you got?' Jeffery Millard's father travelled with him to London when he started as a Gownboy in 1841 to make sure that he settled in. He wrote home to his anxious wife to reassure her that the Matron considered the forty-eight boys in her charge as her own children and that the lads who called into her room while he was there obviously regarded her with great affection; the Matron had taken custody of Jeffery's money, to

Fig 65: A game of cricket played on the Green.
Engraving by Robert Havell after Thomas Ward, 1813.

Photograph courtesy Charterhouse School Archives

be given to him each week and 'every boy has a separate bed and such an one as neither you nor I should object to'. Jeffery added a note of his own on the back of the letter, telling her about the London sights and clearly pleased with his pocket money of sixpence a week.[17] For some, it was all too much: Francis Beaufort Edgeworth begged his mother to take him away a few days after his first arrival in January 1819, writing:

> I am very unhappy and rather ill … At charter house they do not attend much, indeed they scarcely attend to it at all, to writing and arithmetic. I don't thing it is a good school … I have made myself ill in a sort of manner by continual anxiety … Boys swear shockingly … Mr Russel puts too much trust in the monitors. Eating not attended to … The cold is so great that I am often benumbed so that I can scarsly hold my pen … I am your affectionate miserable son FBE.[18]

Presumably Francis settled down, as he stayed at Charterhouse for seven years before going on to Trinity College, Cambridge. John Leech also suffered from homesickness, writing:

> My dear Mamma, I understand that you came to see me yesterday, and me being in the green, you did not see me and that made me still more unhappy, I beg you will come and see me on Saturday for I am very unhappy. I want to see [you] or Papa very much indeed. Your affectionate son, J Leech.[19]

In common with many other public schools, Charterhouse had a fagging system whereby the most junior boys, known as fags, were required to wait on senior boys in their house. Fags were expected to make tea and toast for their seniors, tidy their studies, fetch coal for the fire and be ready to run errands whenever called. Monitors had fags to wait on them in the mornings, known as 'Basinites'. Their duty was to attempt to wake their teenage monitors every ten minutes, having first fetched hot water and towels and laid out clothes ready to be jumped straight into. Inevitably, these wake-up calls were only heeded at the last minute:

> The rush then to get in time was something appalling. A simultaneous scuffle. Basinites ran hither and thither, obedient to shouts of 'My jacket, Jones!', 'Smith, where's my collar?', 'Look sharp now, Tomkins!' (as the latter wretched individual dived into a chaotic mass of waistcoats, shirts, neckties, caps, and gowns thrown into a shapeless heap in the excitement of the moment.

The fagging system was open to abuse and bullying was common. Charles Reynardson was taken away from Charterhouse after a year because he was badly bullied:

> After having been bullied and knocked about, roasted and toasted, tossed in a blanket till I touched the ceiling and burst a hole through the blanket, and was nearly killed by coming in contact with the floor of the long bedroom in which some eight or ten of us slept, I was taken home very ill and was supposed to be going to die. This however I did not do, and, much to my delight, was taken away from the horrible prison and sent to that seat of sound learning and religious education called Eton.[20]

LESSONS

The statutes of 1627 specified that the Schoolmaster should teach only the approved Latin and Greek texts that were studied in the best schools and Charterhouse continued to focus primarily on traditional classical education for the next three centuries. A writing master was employed by the governors to ensure that the younger boys' basic reading and writing skills were developed and boys destined for apprenticeships also studied arithmetic and book-keeping to prepare them for business life, but the main focus was on the classical studies that were essential for entrance to university.

Boys were promoted up the form system depending on their ability rather than their age. William MacPherson arrived at Charterhouse in 1824 and wrote to his father describing his daily routine and his rapid progress: 'I was put by myself to learn the grammar on Monday afternoon, on Thursday when I knew most of it I was put into the eleventh form and on Friday when I had got to the top into the 10th, and today into the ninth, who are doing Latin verses and some Greek sentences in the grammar.' William was a pupil at the height of an educational experiment at Charterhouse, known as the Madras or Bell System. This was a teaching system developed by the Revd Andrew Bell, chaplain to an orphanage in Madras, which enabled one supervisor to teach very large numbers of children by instructing older pupils who then repeated each lesson to the younger ones. The system was taken up in many British elementary schools in order to cope with growing numbers of children in industrial towns. The scheme was introduced at Charterhouse by the Schoolmaster, Dr John Russell, in 1817 and at first it was a great success, with pupil numbers rising from 200 in 1817 to 480 in 1825. The school was divided into twelve forms, each with numerous subdivisions that were supervised by a pupil-teacher known as a 'praeposter'. Promotion was based entirely on merit, not age, with pupils from the top four forms also acting as praeposters. Consequently, a praeposter might be younger and smaller than the pupils he was supervising. Augustus Page Saunders, Schoolmaster from 1832 to 1853, later explained the problems that this could lead to:

There was a praeposter of one form, who, being a little mite but a clever scholar, was put by Dr Russell at the head of his class, but he said it was torture to him above everything; he felt all the responsibilities of his place. Dr Russell would call out, 'Fifth form, where is your praeposter?' 'Please, sir, here he is', and they would hold him up by the neck. You cannot wonder after that that the school fell. [21]

It was easy enough for boys to slip out of school without being noticed and for some to make no progress at all: Henry Liddell (later Dean of Christ Church, Oxford, and the father of the 'real' Alice in Wonderland) was in the same form as William Thackeray and said that Thackeray spent most of his time drawing or reading novels; Thackeray, on the other hand, complained that Liddell had spoilt his chances of academic success by always doing the work for him. With only two classrooms and five masters there came a point when the noise and confusion must have been unmanageable and parents started to withdraw their children. By 1832 numbers at the school had dropped to 137 and Russell resigned. His successor, Dr Saunders, restored a more traditional teaching system and slowly rebuilt the school's reputation.

Gerald Davies went to Charterhouse as a Gownboy in January 1856, aged just ten. He was placed in the most junior form, known as the 'Under Petties', to learn the basic rudiments of Latin. Gerald considered that the Petties' Master, the Revd C. R. Dicken, did not take his role very seriously, as he never appeared in school until 10:00am and then generally reading *The Times* while his charges worked: 'It was our chief ambition to untie Dicken's shoestrings, while he was absorbed in the newspaper, without being found out. Successes to failures were in the proportion of about three to one.' There were still only three classrooms and several lessons could be held simultaneously in the 'Big School', together with other forms who were supposedly preparing their work 'quietly'. Exams were held at the end of Long Quarter (the spring

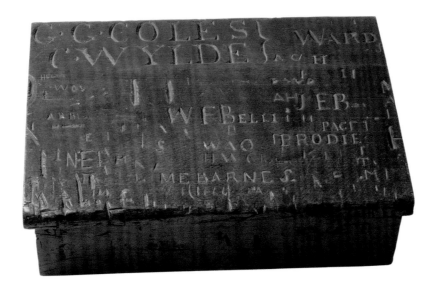

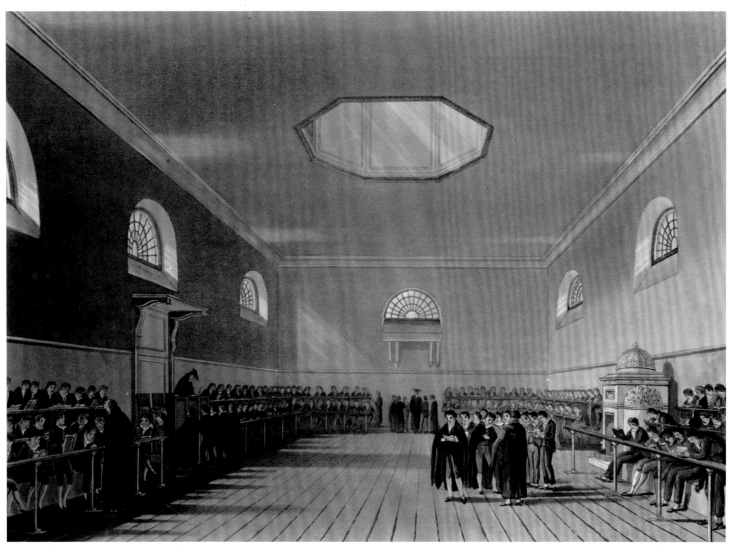

term) and, from 1815 onwards, both the exam papers and the results were printed and sent home to parents. Promotion to the next form depended on passing the exams, with those who struggled academically languishing in junior forms while younger, but abler, boys overtook them. The standard of Latin and Greek scholarship was extremely demanding – every boy in the school was expected to compose verses in Latin – and (by the mid-nineteenth century) basic mathematics, writing, geography, history and divinity were taught to all the junior forms. French, German and chemistry lessons were also offered for an extra fee of 2 guineas a year.

The school day started with prayers in chapel and early lessons, followed by breakfast at 8.30. Lessons resumed at 9.30 until midday and there was then a break for dinner until 2.00pm, followed by two more hours of school. On Wednesdays and Saturdays school ended at midday and there was a half-day holiday, in which boys could play games, take extra classes in drawing, music, fencing or boxing and, if they had permission, go out to visit friends and relatives. Tea was at 7.00pm, and then there was an hour for private study, known as 'Banco'. House prayers were said at 9.00pm by the House Master, who then called the register, with each boy answering 'Adsum' to his name, after which the Under School went to bed. Senior boys could stay up later. This timetable did not allow for much time for games in winter, but it made the most of the daylight hours – a crucial consideration, as there was no lighting in 'Big School', apart from candles.

Order was maintained by harsh discipline: the names of boys misbehaving or failing in their studies were recorded in the 'Black Book' and any boy recorded more than three times within a week would be taken to a room adjacent to 'Big School' and flogged (known as 'swishing') by the Schoolmaster. Boys could also be beaten for refusing to carry out fagging duties, and for many other misdemeanours. Little William MacPherson wrote home fearfully, 'several fellows were flogged today for making a row when they should have been in bed. I expect a turn soon …' Dr Russell tried to abandon flogging and introduce a system of fines instead, but the boys objected on the grounds that fines were 'ungentlemanly' and they would prefer to suffer pain rather than lose their pocket money. Masters and monitors were likely to box the ears of any offending boys and for minor offences extra lines of translation, known as impositions, might be set.

Riots at public schools were not uncommon, and some at Charterhouse were so serious that they were recorded in the governors' Assembly minutes. In 1741 the senior boy (Captain) at Charterhouse had a disagreement with the Gownboy Matron's maid, Susan, who made a complaint about him to the Schoolmaster. As a result, John Roberts was threatened with expulsion and, in revenge, he and the other scholars threw slops and water over her. When the Matron and her women took refuge in her house the scholars broke the windows and demanded that Susan should be thrown out; they continued to riot for several days before order was restored and John Roberts was expelled.[22] Another riot broke out on 12 December 1808 when celebrations at the Founder's Day feast got out of hand, leading once again to the breaking of windows and an attack on the Matron's house, followed by the expulsion of eight boys.

Gerald Davies became Head Monitor in 1864. As part of this role he was required to write a speech or 'oration' in Latin, which he had to learn by heart and deliver to guests at Founder's Day on 12 December. The autumn term at Charterhouse is still called 'Oration Quarter', although the current Head Monitor is no longer required to speak in Latin. At the end of the speech, the orator would hold out his mortar board so that the audience could place donations in it. Gerald Davies went up to Christ's College, Cambridge, in 1865 with a substantial nest egg from his oration collection, plus a Charterhouse Exhibition of £80 per annum, paid for four years; he also won a Talbot Gold Medal and

Fig 66: **A wooden box made from the remains of a 'mobbed' school desk.**

Photograph courtesy Charterhouse School Archives

Fig 67: **The new school room at the Charterhouse.** Print from Rudolph Ackermann's *The History of the Colleges ...etc* (London, 1816).

Photograph courtesy Charterhouse School Archives

Fig 68: **The school's first XI football team, 1863.**

Photograph courtesy Charterhouse School Archives

£72, awarded by Charterhouse for classical scholarship. Davies returned to Charterhouse in Godalming in 1873 as an assistant master and was the founder of 'Daviesites' boarding house and of the school museum; after retiring as a schoolmaster he then became Master of the London Charterhouse.

Some musical instruction was provided, as the chapel organist had always been required to teach the Gownboys to sing and many of the fee-paying pupils also opted to join the singing practice twice a week. Not only did the boys sing at chapel services, but a popular annual concert was held in the Great Hall every May. Gerald Davies described the organist in his time, John Hullah, as 'one of the most cultured and most fascinating of men', who set many of Charles Kingsley's poems to music for the boys to sing for the first time at the School concert: 'It was a rich treat when Hullah, before the arrival of the body of the class, would, to a favoured few of us, sing over one of these new settings in his fine baritone voice'. Another former pupil remembered Hullah as 'a strikingly handsome man … with curly iron-grey hair and refined and intellectual features'.[23]

Drawing classes were also available for those boys whose parents chose to pay extra, with Drawing Masters who were talented and inspiring artists. Boys such as William Thackeray and John Leech found an outlet for their creativity that was lacking from the rest of the school curriculum. Leech showed an extraordinary talent from a very young age, particularly in his remarkably accurate drawings of horses. His Latin textbook is full of humorous illustrations of the exercises that provide a lively insight into school life.[24] (Figs. 72, 73, 74)

SPORT

Parents could pay for professional fencing or boxing lessons, but all other sporting activities were organised informally by the boys themselves. Football developed at Charterhouse as a mob game that could include any number of players. It was played in two forms: 'runabout', which was an outdoor game focusing on dribbling skills and recognisable as a form of today's Association football; and an indoor game played in the cloisters in which two opposing teams formed mass scrums to push the ball towards doors at either end of the cloister corridor. Games involving the whole school, with Gownboys playing against the rest, were not uncommon, and must have been a terrifying experience for the smaller, less robust boys. The fags acted as group goalkeepers while the rest of the school chased the ball until, inevitably, it got caught in one of the buttresses, leading to a huddle of fifty or sixty boys, all kicking and shoving to reach the ball:

> A skilful player … would dexterously work out the ball and rush wildly with it down Cloisters towards the coveted goal. The squash would then dissolve and go in pursuit. Now was the time for the pluck and judgement of the Fags to be tried. To prevent the ball getting in amongst them at the goal, one of the foremost Fags would rush out and engage the onset of the dribbling foe, generally to be sent spinning head over heels for five yards along the stones … One of these scrimmages sometimes lasted three-quarters of an hour. Shins would be kicked black and blue; jackets and other articles of clothing almost torn in to shreds; and Fags trampled under foot.[25]

The first recorded match against an external team was played against Dingley Dell in October 1862. In 1863 the 1st XI captain attended the inaugural meeting of the Football Association, taking with him Charterhouse's football rules. Other team captains, including Westminster School, came with their football rules and the FA regulations were drawn up as an amalgamation of these various versions of the game.[26]

Cricket was also popular, although Westminster School rejected

Henry Herschel Hay Cameron
  as
Reuben Goldschoel.

an invitation to play against Charterhouse in 1818 on the grounds that their players were very inferior and also that it was considered beneath Westminster to accept a challenge from a private school.[27] Carthusian cricketers certainly lacked the space and facilities to develop their skills: the only playground space was the square within the cloisters known as 'Green'(Fig. 65), which was not much more than 100 square metres. In 1819 Dr Russell complained that this over-used area was uneven, full of holes and quite unsuitable for playing games. After a two-year battle he finally won approval from the governors to level and 'improve' Green and also to remove a wall separating Green from the old monastic 'Wilderness' garden to create an extra playground, which was renamed as 'Under Green'.

Some hockey was played, generally by the younger boys, and there was also an early form of Racquets, described as 'Bat-Fives', played with long wooden bats in a court consisting of two walls. 'Hoops' was also a popular game, entailing spinning a large wooden or metal hoop along the ground. 'Hoops were always driven, or as we called it, "tooled", in pairs, with a very light stick, and to perform this feat neatly required considerable practice. When the hoop season went out it was the custom to fling the hoops up into the trees, the more completely out of reach the better.'[27] Hoops were raced around the perimeter of Green, negotiating corners and obstacles and finishing at a point on the east wall where the word 'Crown' had been painted to represent the nearby Crown coaching inn where stagecoaches stopped to drop off visitors to Charterhouse.

The lack of supervision led to even rougher 'games' that were effectively full-scale battles. The annual 'Lemon Peel Fight' took place on Shrove Tuesday, when boys would save the half-lemons issued to them with their pancakes and pelt each other with them: Gownboys against the rest of the school. Far more violent was the Good Friday 'Pulling Out', a battle between the Under School and the Uppers (senior boys) in which the Unders could call out any unpopular Upper

to run the gauntlet through them from the cloister doors to a point near the chapel. This custom came to an abrupt end in 1824 when one of the smallest boys, twelve-year-old John Howard, was trampled and killed in a stampede.

DRAMA

Amateur dramatics had always been encouraged, often written by the boys themselves, with titles such as 'A Dramatic Piece: by the Charter-House Scholars: in Memory of the Powder-Plot. Performed at the Charter-House, November 6th 1732' or 'Bubble and Squeak, the Charterhouse Play', performed in 1844. William Haig Brown introduced annual school plays, to which friends and family could be invited, with tickets in high demand. Alfred Saunders wrote to his sister before one such performance:

> I don't know when I shall be able to come home because the theatricals are on Saturday night and old Poynder objects to travelling on a Sunday, so I suppose I shall have to stop here until the Monday, which will be very low. I suppose Mrs Haig Brown has sent you some tickets. If you don't want them, you may send them to me.

The following year he wrote, 'I suppose none of you will be going to Theatricals this year. If not, will you please send me any tickets which Mrs Haig [Brown] may have sent you, because I want them very much indeed.'

A printed programme was produced for the Charterhouse theatricals of December 1868, with acknowledgements to a commercial costumier and a hairdresser; two comedies were performed, 'Payable on Demand' by Tom Taylor and 'The Bengal Tiger' by Charles Dance, with boys playing both male and female parts. Press reports were published and the main characters were photographed (Fig. 69).

Fig 69: Henry Herschel Hay Cameron playing Reuben Goldsched in *Payable on Demand* by Tom Taylor, produced at Charterhouse in December 1868. He was the son of photographer Julia Margaret Cameron.

Photograph courtesy Charterhouse School Archives

Register of the doings

of

E. C. C.

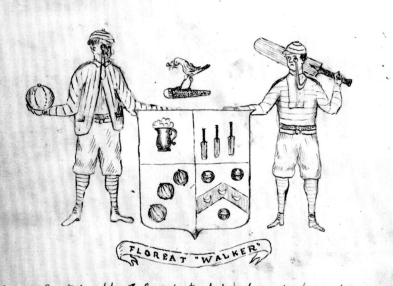

FLOREAT "WALKER"

2d Burg Cault

Arms Quarterly 1st. Gules a pewter pot proper with foam d'argent handle
sinister side. Second Vert three cricket bats palewise proper. Third. Vert. Three
bend sinister proper. 4th Or. on a cheveron gules three crescents of first b
ree cricket balls of the second.

Crest Jack D'or with strawberry pottle couchant. holding in his
cherry proper.

upporters. Dexter Sinister. Cricketer Rampant. with bat proper in sinist
exter. Football player. guardant. Holding football improper in dexter
ott in club colours. and Knickerbockers proper

THE EPICURE CLUB

The Epicure Club was invented by Gerald Davies and his schoolfriends to amuse themselves and to 'take the mickey' out of other similar groups that took themselves more seriously. The society's minute book provides an insight into informal schoolboy interests and humour that is lacking from other records: recording informal sports matches, concerts and theatricals in which society members performed ridiculous turns. Members had nicknames, such as 'Miss Martha Podge-Mackintosh' (Montague Muir Mackenzie), 'Lord Bung Caulk' (John Morice Byng; Fig. 71) and 'the Marquis de Hibernia' (the Hon. Frederick Standish O'Grady). They invented their own coat of arms, featuring a jackdaw as their mascot (Fig. 70), and printed a long list of silly rules: 'If a player lose his temper he shall be required to find it again immediately – or he may stick up a notice' and 'If a player knock another down he must wait till he gets up again before repeating the operation'. The butler of Gownboys and the Matron of Verites were honorary members of the club.

Epicure sports matches were played against other teams within Charterhouse, including their arch rivals, the Stoics Club. Match reports were quirky and might include features such as the varying styles of knickerbockers worn by the contestants rather than a football commentary. One cricket match with Epicures against the rest of the School was played with the Epicures using hockey sticks instead of bats. The Epicures held a 'Race Meeting' on 24 October 1864 to celebrate the festival of their patron saint, 'St Walker', and wrote a twelve-page imaginative report: 'a Grand Stand was erected at a great expense and was crammed with spectators including many of the fair sex, while banners floated in the breeze and the softest music charmed the savage breasts of a large collection of masters. (NB the band consisted of the Marquis de Hibernia, accompanied by his trumpet).' Races included the 50 yards Blindfold Stakes, the VI Form 100 yards Handicap or

Charterhouse 'Oax' (won by 'Crazy Jane') and the Epicure Handicap, won by 'Miss Martha'. Epicure concerts were held in the Gownboys Hall and featured popular songs and instrumental pieces of dubious quality, including solo performances on the triangle and the concertina. Miss Martha's cello performance was described as producing such lifelike groans and screams that the audience imagined the instrument to be in great pain.

THE MOVE TO GODALMING

In 1861 the Government set up the Clarendon Commission to scrutinise education in the nine great public schools, including Charterhouse. The Commission's report in 1864 included the radical recommendation that the School should move out of London to a healthier environment for its pupils. The governing body and William Hale, the Master (in overall charge of both the Brothers and the School), vehemently opposed the move and feared the consequences of splitting the two parts of Sutton's foundation. However, the recently appointed Schoolmaster, William Haig Brown, favoured moving, both for the sake of the pupils' well-being and, perhaps, to escape from the interference of the Master in school affairs. He canvassed four hundred Old Carthusians and won their overwhelming approval for the move, after which the governors were persuaded to reconsider. They specified that the new school site must be in the south of England, within three miles of a town, between 30 and 100 acres, and within easy reach of water for boating. Various sites were considered, including Little Hallingbury in Essex, where Thomas Sutton had originally planned to locate his foundation, but the final choice was the Deanery Farm Estate at Godalming, purchased for £9450. The terms of Thomas Sutton's foundation had to be altered to allow the School to move and this was finally approved by Act of Parliament in August 1867. Merchant Taylors' School in London was looking for new premises and purchased part of the London

Fig 70: Drawing in the Epicure Club's minute book. The club's coat of arms incorporate a 'cricketer rampant holding bat proper' and 'football player guardant with football improper', 1864.

Photograph courtesy Charterhouse School Archives

Fig 71: Lord Bung Caulk, a drawing in the Epicure Club's minute book, 1864.

Photograph courtesy Charterhouse School Archives

Charterhouse site for £90,000 ; this financed the building of the new Charterhouse at Godalming, designed by Philip Hardwick.

The pupils who arrived from London on 18 June 1872 must have been overwhelmed by the contrast with the hubbub, crowds and pollution of Victorian London. They travelled by steam train and would have alighted at the Charterhouse siding between Farnborough and Godalming stations. Luggage was carried up the hill by horse and cart, while the boys followed on foot along Peperharow Road with fields and market gardens on either side. Within a few years the main access into the School moved to a shorter and more convenient route via Charterhouse Road, but in 1872 this was just a farm track known as Sandy Lane. Compared to the noise, smells and bustle of Smithfield, the empty countryside, the quietness and fresh air must have seemed quite unnerving to some. As they reached the crest of Racquets Court Hill the boys must surely have been impressed by the grand Gothic vista of the new Charterhouse. However, there were elements of the new school that would have been familiar: Philip Hardwick's brief had been to replicate the buildings of the old school, so there were three boarding Houses with the familiar names of Saunderites, Verites and Gownboys and there was a large hall (now the Library) with six classrooms off it. There was accommodation for Housemasters and their families in the 'Private Side' of each House, there was a Masters' Common Room, and there were even cloisters reminiscent of the old monastic buildings. Finally there was a chapel, although this was not completed until March 1874.

Gownboys at the London Charterhouse could pay to have their names carved into the stone doorway that originally led from Scholars' Court into the Gownboys building: former pupils' names were also carved into the facing of the 'Big School', built in 1803. Rather than lose these historic carvings, the stones were dismantled and reconstructed in Godalming between the Chapel and Gownboys House. Long-established Carthusian names were replicated in Godalming to provide a sense of continuity: Brooke Hall, Green, Under Green, Crown, Big Ground, Wilderness, Scholars' Court and Middle Briars.

During the summer of 1872 the pupils explored their new surroundings. A cricket pitch had been cleared and laid with turf, but was not ready to be used, and the future 1st XI football pitch ('Big Ground') was still 'a wild tangle of gorse, yellow broom and blue borage'. Instead of playing sports the boys were encouraged to explore and swim in the River Wey at the foot of the hill. In central London few had learnt to swim and A. H. Tod recalled that one monitor nearly drowned: 'twice he sank, but on coming up for the third time he fortunately recollected his monitorial privileges and shouted "Fag", a happy thought which probably saved his life, for fags came promptly and rescued him.'[29] Swimming lessons were soon introduced for all pupils, the bathing place on the river was improved with a concrete edge and changing cubicles and a swimming supervisor was appointed. Although the river was not wide enough for serious rowing, other water activities were encouraged, with entertaining canoe and tub races presided over by the Headmaster himself.[30]

One of those boys who transferred from the London Charterhouse to Godalming was Robert Baden-Powell. He revelled in the freedom and in later life recalled that it was here, in the 'School of the Copse', that he first discovered his love of the outdoor skills that were to become a key feature of his Scouting for Boys movement:

> I learned to creep silently and to 'freeze' (i.e. to stay motionless), to find my way by land marks, to notice tracks and read their meaning, to use dry, dead wood off trees (and not off the damp ground) for my fire, to make a tiny non-smokey fire such as would not give me away to prying masters; and if these came along I had my sod of turf ready to extinguish the fire and hide the spot while I shinned up a neighbouring ivy-clad tree where I could nestle unobserved above the line of sight of the average searcher.[31]

By contrast, in London every building and tree was so blackened with coal smoke that climbing a tree would have covered the climber with soot.[32]

The school was constructed out of Bargate sandstone, dug from a quarry within the Charterhouse site. Although the basic buildings were finished by June 1872 the internal fabric and fittings were far from complete and, apart from beds, most of the furniture had not arrived, so pupils and staff were basically camping for the first few weeks, with a blacksmith's forge running all night in the Verite lower dormitory and stonemasons working on the chapel. The buildings were infested with earwigs and rats, so the boys were allowed to keep pet ferrets to get rid of the rats. The only lighting came from candles until the gas lighting could be installed.[33]

One hundred and fifty pupils had arrived in Godalming in June 1872, of whom 117 were existing pupils from the old Charterhouse. The new facilities and the healthy environment met with the approval of parents and pupil numbers accordingly rose very rapidly, reaching 500 in 1876. This unexpected success caused an accommodation crisis and Masters with private means were therefore encouraged to buy adjacent land and set up their own privately run boarding houses, each named after its founding Housemaster. Seven boarding houses were established in this way and extra classrooms and facilities were added gradually over the next twenty years. William Haig Brown acted as project manager for all the building work in addition to his other roles as Headmaster, Bursar and Housemaster of Saunderites. Not for nothing is he known as the second founder of Charterhouse, as he had succeeded in re-establishing the School in a new setting, whilst preserving many of its old traditions and keeping strong links with the Brothers of the London Charterhouse. He retired in 1897, returning back to London as Master of Sutton's Hospital, leaving a well-established and successful school in Godalming.

Fig 72: **Doodles by John Leech in his Latin textbook, some illustrating the grammatical rules he was supposed to be studying.**

Photograph courtesy Charterhouse School Archives

210. No letter comes WITHOUT a SUBJECT.
211. Cæsar wept BEFORE the SENATE.
212. Æneas comes WITH his son.
213. Philosophers argue CONCERNING this MATTER.
214. I have watched FROM the CALENDS of January.
215. Thou art happy IN-COMPARISON-OF US.
216. Cicero had made the speech FOR ARCHIAS.
217. No man is found altogether WITHOUT FAULTS.
218. The king was sitting ON the THRONE.
219. The reward will be given UNDER that CONDITION.
220. I have spoken UPON this SUBJECT.

RULE XI.

A Verb of the INDICATIVE MOOD either ASSERTS, or DENIES; or it is used in ASKING a QUESTION.

221. Vita bene acta senectutem jucundam REDDIT.
       Reddit, Indicative Verb, asserting.
222. Superbi homines non STABUNT.
223. Quando nos hominem INVENIEMUS parem?
224. Labor CONQUERS the most difficult things.
225. The good shepherd NEGLECTS not his sheep.
226. When shall I behold THEE?

RULE XII.

A Verb of the SUBJUNCTIVE MOOD is used in sentences SUB-JOINED TO, or dependent on another sentence.

The Dependent Sentence has generally some Conjunction, or Relative set before it.

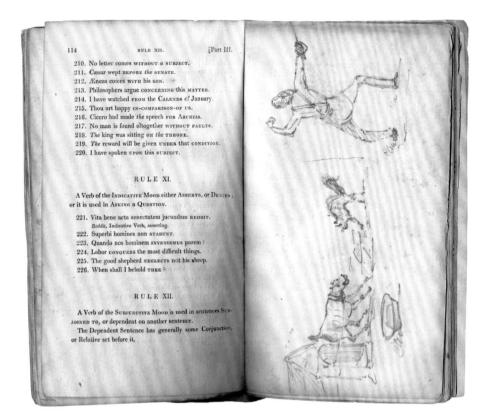

A Noun expressing the WHOLE, *of which* PART *is taken, is in the Genitive with the Adjective, that marks the* PART.

122. Primus REGUM Romanorum erat Romulus.

     "*Regum,*" genitive, used with "*primus.*"

123. EORUM ut quisque primus venerat, sub muro consiste-bat.

The Substantives "PROPERTY," "PART," "DUTY," "SIGN," *used in English after the Verb* AM, *are omitted in turning the sentence into Latin.*

124. To obey is the duty of a SON.
125. To die for his country is the part of a BRAVE MAN.

     "*It concerns*" *may be turned into Latin by the word* "*interest*" *or* "*refert,*" *the* PERSON *being in the* GENITIVE *case.*

126. *It* concerns CLODIUS, that Milo *should* perish.
127. *It* concerns the REPUBLIC, that there be two consuls.
128. This concerns not THOSE persons.
129. This concerned thee much.   "*Thine much among was.*"
130. I condemn others of INACTIVITY.
131. *We* remember *our* ancient FAME.
132. *Thou* wilt recollect thy OFFENCES with some sorrow.
133. He will be grieved at his FOLLY.   "*Him will grieve.*"
134. We are weary of LIFE.   "*Weariness of life wearies us.*"
135. Pity a MIND bearing *things* not deserved.
136. Cicero was greedy of GLORY.
137. *I* hate *a* man unmindful of KINDNESSES.
138. The queen is rich in CATTLE.
139. Cæsar calls out to him the first men of the GAULS.
140. Miltiades was most singularly distinguished *above* ALL.

References

1 See Gerald S Davies, *Charterhouse in London: Monastery, Mansion, Hospital, School* (London, 1921) for a good overview of the school.

2 Ibid., 257.

3 'Moseley', 'Horae Carta-Casianae by Suttonides' [an account of life at Charterhouse School], *Northampton Mercury* (n.d. [1820–25]), Charterhouse School Archive [Ch. Arc.] 182/1/3,.

4 Davies, *Charterhouse in London*, 256.

5 A. H. Tod, *Charterhouse* (London, 1900), 113.

6 Davies, *Charterhouse in London*, 288.

7 Stephen Porter, *The London Charterhouse* (Stroud, 2009).

8 Barker brothers' bills, 1823–4, Ch. Arc. 0376.

9 E. P. Eardley-Wilmot and E. C. Streatfield, *Charterhouse Old and New* (London, 1895), 94.

10 Revd H. L. Thompson, *Henry George Liddell … a Memoir* (London, 1899), 5.

11 Davies, *Charterhouse in London*, 202.

12 Valentine letter from Lovick Henry Cooper to sister of William John Lewis, 1843–9, Ch. Arc. 0380.

13 Eardley-Wilmot and Streatfield, *Charterhouse Old and New*, 80.

14 Letter from Dr Crusius to Revd Lushington at Eastbourne, 26 Dec. 1754, Ch. Arc. 0371.

15 See n. 3.

16 Eardley-Wilmot and Streatfield, *Charterhouse Old and New*, 63.

17 Letter from Jeffery Millard at Charterhouse to his mother, March 1841, Ch. Arc. 0176.

18 R. A. Arrowsmith, *A Charterhouse Miscellany* (London, 1982).

19 Letters by John Leech from school, Ch. Arc. 018.

20 C.T.S. Birch Reynardson, *Down the Road, or Reminiscences of a Gentleman Coachman* (London, 1875), 11.

21 Public Schools Commission 1862, Minutes of Evidence, Charterhouse.

22 'The Gownboy Rebellion of 1741', *The Carthusian* (July 1953).

23 Eardley-Wilmot and Streatfield, *Charterhouse Old and New*, 106.

24 *Rudiments of the Latin Language for the use of Charterhouse School*, Ch. Arc. 102/2.

25 Eardley-Wilmot and Streatfield, *Charterhouse Old and New*, 75.

26 Malcolm Bailey, *From Cloister to Cup Finals: a History of Charterhouse Football* (Shrewsbury, 2008).

27 Westminster School, 'The Town Boy Ledgers', August 1818, available at http://townboyledger.westminster.org.uk (accessed 17 March 2016).

28 See n. 3.

29 Tod, *Charterhouse*, 77.

30 'Aquatics', *The Carthusian* (July and October 1873).

31 Robert Baden-Powell, *The Greyfriar*, XVIII, no.123 (December 1927).

32 'Random Rememberings', *The Carthusian* (July 1884).

33 Tod, *Charterhouse*, chapters II and III.

Figs 73, 74: **Doodles by John Leech in his Latin textbook, some illustrating the grammatical rules he was supposed to be studying.**

Photograph courtesy Charterhouse School Archives

Following pages:

Fig 75: **Gravestones in chapel cloister.**

Photograph by Lawrence Watson

a day in the life
of the Charterhouse
3: afternoon

12.55	Bell rings for the Brothers' lunch served at 1.00pm in the great hall.
2.00–4.30	Various activities: some Brothers lead guided tours around the Charterhouse. Film companies may arrive (the buildings are in demand as a film set).
3.45	Brothers' tea in the great hall.
4.45	End of public opening hours.
5.30	Evening prayers in the chapel (open to the public). Day staff leave; the infirmary's night staff arrive.
DUSK	The Charterhouse flag is lowered.

The Architecture

Eric Parry

Several excellent books and a multitude of academic papers exist to celebrate the extraordinary richness of the Charterhouse – until now one of London's best-kept secrets. It now finds itself needing to secure a fiscal future whilst also being thrust into one of the capital city's new twenty-first century transport interchanges. This essay is not an exhaustive description of the buildings; it rather seeks to highlight some of the architectural character that has been so interestingly reshaped many times for changing social needs over six and a half centuries. Indeed the way in which the common theme of 'dwelling' has been able to fit into the physical fabric is a lesson in reuse, adaptation and, above all, learning from the buildings and the site bequeathed to us. It is a fascinating and rather humbling lesson in the pell-mell of a rapidly changing contemporary city – London.

PLACE AND CONTEXT

Standing at the position where the new gateway to the square will be, opposite the Elizabeth Line station entrance, looking north to the southern elevation of the Charterhouse the fabric of buildings is broken by a dense foliage section with railings and a mysterious private garden beyond. This view is framed by the canopy of the mature plane trees and their massive trunks. It is an unusual space of deep repose in this densely occupied part of London, typically undercut by infrastructure and girdled by busy roads. This verdant space marks a point of equilibrium between the east and west of the trapezoid square and forms an unseen ley line that heralds the hidden world beyond, a length of more than three hundred metres to Clerkenwell Road, around which the shadow of the fourteenth-century Carthusian monastery persists.

This gap is indeed a resonant one, exposed by the destruction of two houses facing the square by bomb damage in 1942. It is more so because it lies on what was the sacred communal heart of the Carthusian monastery, the priory church. This was itself flanked to the north by smaller chapels dedicated to St Catherine, St Agnes and the chapter-house (which forms the principal volume of today's Sutton's Hospital in Charterhouse's chapel) and to the south by chapels dedicated to St Michael, St John the Baptist, St Jerome, St Bernard and St John the Evangelist. Conjectured also at or near the point of today's railings was a pulpit house to address, one imagines, the lay community in what was known as the New Church Hawe, the amalgam of Pardon Churchyard, which was consecrated during the plague year of 1348, and an adjacent ground known as the Spital Croft. Following the 1348 outbreak and prior to the Carthusian monastery's foundation in 1371, Ralph Stratford. Bishop of London, had had a small chapel erected where masses were celebrated for the dead. This is probably the root of the ecclesiastical building illustrated in a later state at the centre of the space named Charterhouse on the early 'Agas Map' of London (c.1560). This plan marks the sites of intervention for the 'Revealing the Charterhouse' project, discussed in this essay within the greater context of the outstanding complex of buildings that make up the whole site (Fig. 77).

The shadow of the Carthusian foundation is a remarkable and precious survivor, particularly because of its proximity to the City of London. Pleasure gardens from the seventeenth century to the nineteenth, for instance, with their fragile footprints, once full of life and gossip, have been universally obliterated by subsequent development as they were also set in close proximity to their urban catchment. Every century from its fourteenth-century foundation has brought the threat of erasure resulting from fiscal pressure, political turmoil or the upheavals and opportunities of urban planning, and yet its foundation is still clearly outlined today. When the monastery was originally laid out in 1371 for twenty-four monks and a prior, which in Carthusian terms was a double house requiring a layout to suit this ambition, the design was admirably delivered by the architect-mason

Fig 76: **The north side of Wash-house Court, as seen from the laundry room.**

Photograph by Lawrence Watson

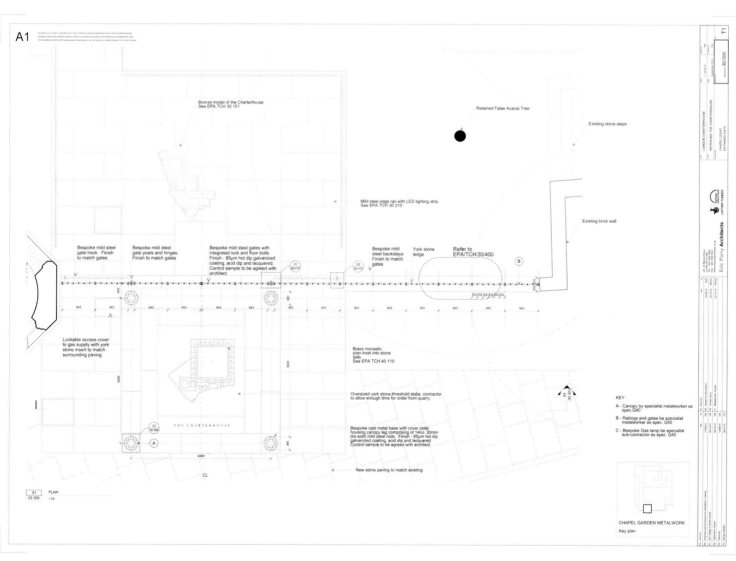

A1

Bronze model of the Charterhouse
See EPA TCH 30 101

Retained False Acacia Tree

Existing stone steps

Mild steel edge rail with LED lighting strip.
See EPA TCH 30 210

Existing brick wall

Bespoke mild steel
gate hook. Finish
to match gates

Bespoke mild steel
gate posts and hinges.
Finish to match gates

Bespoke mild steel gates with
integrated lock and floor bolts.
Finish - 85μm hot dip galvanized
coating, acid dip and lacquered.
Control sample to be agreed with
architect

Bespoke mild
steel backstays
Finish to match
gates

York stone
ledge

Refer to
EPA/TCH/30/400

B

Lockable access cover
to gas supply with york
stone insert to match
surrounding paving

Brass monastic
plan inset into stone
slab.
See EPA TCH 40 110

THE CHARTERHOUSE

Oversized york stone threshold slabs. contractor
to allow enough time for order from quarry.

Bespoke cast metal base with cover plate
housing canopy leg comprising of 14no. 30mm
dia solid mild steel rods. Finish - 85μm hot dip
galvanized coating, acid dip and lacquered.
Control sample to be agreed with architect

A

New stone paving to match existing

CL

KEY:

A - Canopy by specialist metalworker as
spec. Q40

B - Railings and gates be specialist
metalworker as spec. Q40

C - Bespoke Gas lamp be specialist
sub-contractor as spec. Q40

01   PLAN
03 300   1:25

Eric Parry Architects

LONDON CHARTERHOUSE
REVEALING THE CHARTERHOUSE
CHAPEL COURT
ENTRANCE GATE

30 300

T1

CHAPEL GARDEN METALWORK
Key plan

Henry Yevele. It would seem he worked within a square outline plan, 136 × 136 metres, within which he planned a cloistered rectangle, 95 × 85 metres, offset northwards within the greater square to accommodate the depth of the communal buildings and the chapel to the south, facing onto the open ground of the Church Hawe.

The depth of the disciplined architectural imagination behind this superficially simple outline, represented in the brass inlay under the canopy of the new entrance, can be grasped better when one understands that Henry Yevele was also the author, among many other works, of the nave of Canterbury Cathedral, which is incontestably the finest architectural space of the fourteenth century in southern England. Fifty years after the beginning of the monastic building phase, the completion of the chapter-house ensured the priory's essential needs were fulfilled. By the time of the Reformation the Charterhouse had taken its place as one of an almost continuous line of monastic properties extending from the north bank of the Thames to Clerkenwell. Two broadly parallel roads from the north form a closer rectangle, that to the west leading through the St John's Gate to Smithfield, while the other to the east became Goswell Road, leading to Aldersgate and beyond to St Paul's.

What is most striking about this plan is how geometric and precise the open space of the Carthusian monastic cloister is. It forms a harmonious square in a sea of tumbling irregular boundaries, finding another moment of repose in the axiality and scale of St Paul's Cathedral to the south. It is certainly one of the largest enclosed spaces in medieval London. This repose is a precise urban manifestation of the Carthusian motto: *Stat crux dum volvitur orbis* ('the cross stands while the world turns'). The order founded by St Bruno in 1084 includes male and female branches and, rather than a rule, abides by its statutes, which abound with the praise of solitude, meditation and silence:

Our supreme quest and goal is to find God in solitude and silence. There, indeed, as a man with his friend, do the Lord and his servant often speak together; there is the faithful soul frequently united with the Word of God; there is the bride made one with her spouse; there is earth joined to heaven, the divine to the human. Commonly, however, the journey is long, and the way dry and barren, that must be travelled to attain the font of living water (Statutes 11.12.1).

Each Charterhouse consists of a community of religious men, known in the case of a monastery as choir monks. Each has their own cell consisting of a lower floor for workshop and store, as monks engage in manual labour, and an upper level consisting of an oratory, a bed, a desk and a table for eating meals. Each cell has a high walled garden. The choir monks are supported by lay brothers who live a more communal life, sharing a common area of the Charterhouse and providing assistance to the choir monks from books to managing supplies. As far as is feasible the hermit choir monks have no contact with the outside world: their contribution to the world is their missionary life of silence and prayer. From this briefest of summaries of a complex and subtle order the layout that they bequeathed to London becomes legible: the ideal precinct surrounded by cells, bounded in many cases to the south by communal buildings, a further common territory for the lay brothers and then the umbilical connection to the world outside. So it is in London. The main surviving elements of the pre-Reformation buildings are the lay brothers' quarters surrounding Wash-house Court (Fig. 76), which with its walls and even its floor creates a vivid picture of the hard-working, down-to-earth support for the structured idealism of the monastic world. The other survivor is the main gate and adjacent wall, set to mediate between the four-square plan of the monastery and the more chaotic pressures of the city, formerly pastures and burial fields outside. With these few elements, together with the chapter-house,

Fig 77: **The scope of the 'Revealing the Charterhouse' project, 2016, shaded in yellow.**

Courtesy Eric Parry Architects

Fig 78: **Plan of the new entrance, marking the floor inlay and the cast-model showing, respectively, the medieval great cloister and the site today.**

Courtesy Eric Parry Architects

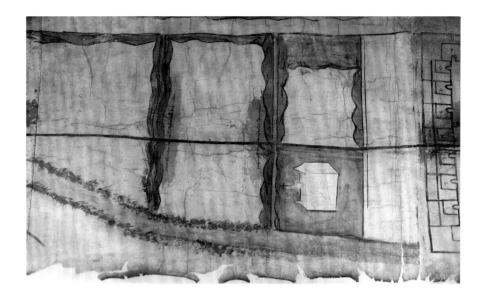

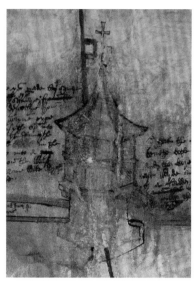

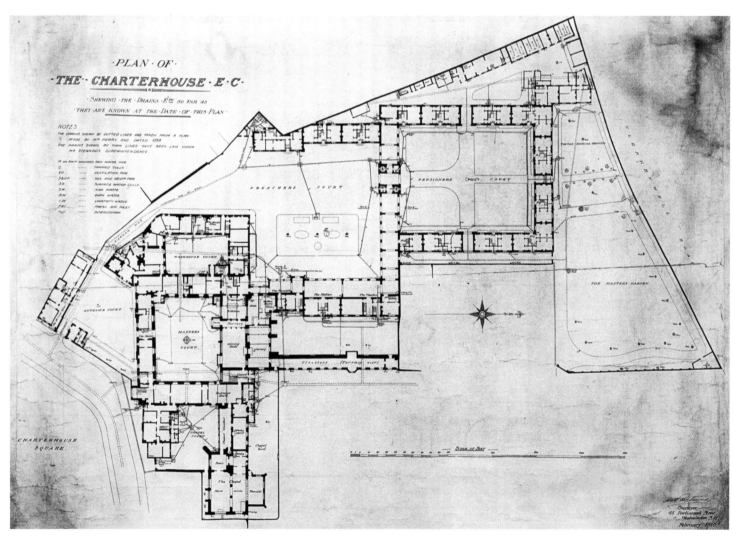

the outline of the precinct and the doorways to several cells embedded in the later fabric, the Charterhouse in London is still very much in evidence as the founding layers of the 'Revealing' project.

THE GUIDING PRESENCE OF WATER

Architecture is an art form inextricably bound up with the pragmatics and physicality of the material world and yet, as the soaring shafts and spreading vaults of Yevele's Canterbury Cathedral have illustrated, the synthesis of a stone framework and the dematerialised walls of glass bear witness to the presence of Christianity in the medieval world of architecture. Freshness, surprise and invention are the gift of great architecture, laying out the possible for future interpretation. Another material example of the interdependence of thought and matter or poetics and pragmatics is the presence of living water. As critical as the formal rectitude of the architectural layout of a monastery, governed by an order's guidance of precedent and rule, was the supply of water. Water is after all one of the four fundamental elements, the others being earth, air and fire, the source of continuity in much classical and medieval philosophical speculation.

At the Charterhouse, water supply was secured after 1430, sourced from higher ground in Clerkenwell from an area later called White Conduit Fields – possibly a reference to the white wool habits of Carthusian monks. The agreement to bury pipework through and under other land ownerships was made along with an endowment for repair and maintenance. Once within the precinct water was stored in a cistern in a conduit house (Fig. 80). One of the most remarkable aids to 'revealing' the Charterhouse is the water supply plan of about 1450, which indicates the main supply from the north branching to each side of the precinct. The water touches on both sacred and secular, from the liturgical use of water, to the Brewhouse tank, kitchen, cistern and so on along with terminals, together with interceptors and other important junctions. The joined vellum sheets that make up the whole, illustrated with drawings of parts together with further notation, give the clearest extant information about the completed priory. These medieval drawings of plumbing are vital to understanding the architecture of a precise period. At Canterbury the highly sophisticated, colour-coded drawing of the waterworks shows the Norman priory as a bird's-eye projection in great detail before the devastating fire of 1174. Drawn in ink, it appears as two facing folios in a manuscript in Trinity College, Cambridge known as the Eadwine Psalter. From it the direction of water flow can be understood by the colour coding: green for fresh water, orange red for water that has passed through the central cistern, red for sewage, and brown for rainwater. The central water tower and cistern still stands at Canterbury and, along with the over-scaled representation of the same type of small building on the fifteenth-century plan of the Charterhouse, gives a clear impression of what the Charterhouse conduit house would have been.

While the changing nature of the architecture is patent across time, two of the most constant issues are the firmness of foundations and the drawing in of clean and the disposal of soiled water. In this respect a 1910 plan of the drains at Sutton's Hospital (Fig. 81) has a striking resemblance of purpose to its fifteenth-century counterpart 'shewing the drains etc. so far as they are known at the date of this plan'. The plan of 1910 is notated in the same way and with the same apprehension: 'the drains shown by dotted lines are taken from a plan made by Mr Perry and dated 1884. The drains shewn by firm lines have been laid under Mr Steward's superintendence.' In the same cryptic key, interceptors, trapped gullies and surface water gullies are all carefully shown for the sake of those responsible for the future upkeep of the site and buildings. As the fifteenth-century plan shows, pipes travelled north, south, east and west from the conduit house, running under the middle of each range to feed the courtyard garden spaces surrounding the two-storeyed cells.

Fig 79: Detail from the fifteenth-century drawing of the Charterhouse's water system showing the main pipe entering the cloister: also see fig 20.

Fig 80: Detail from the fifteenth-century drawing of the Charterhouse's water system showing the central conduit house: also see fig 20.

Fig 81: Plan showing the drains and water system at the Charterhouse, 1910.

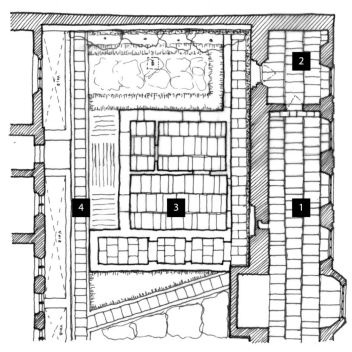

1 Norfolk Cloister
2 Privy Garden Room
3 Monks' Cells' Garden
4 Water Rill

The scale of the individual monks' buildings, each probably with a chimney and about 25 feet square, would have been in stark contrast to the grandeur of the precinct and covered way. This contrast of scale is evoked in spirit by visiting the Grande Chartreuse, the great founding monastery of the Carthusian order, north of Grenoble, which was founded by the hermit St Bruno in 1084, and a closer equivalent, the late fourteenth-century Certosa di Pavia, south of Milan, where the large cloister (125 × 100 metres) has similar proportions but is a little larger than that in London. Particular to the order is the necessary thickness of the precinct wall to accommodate the 'turn', a small opening, curved in plan, adjacent to the cell door, to enable meals and other items to be passed to and fro without the hermit having to encounter human presence directly.

The first radical transformation of the monastic buildings followed the savage suppression of the order by Henry VIII and his henchman Thomas Cromwell. The buildings were stripped of any valuable trappings, lead, glass, panelling and the great belfry clock. The site was used as a workshop and store for the King's tents – a mobile town of about 200 prefabricated buildings – more or less a builder's yard. Additionally there were ad hoc tenancies included, a recorder consort who took up lodgings and, by this date, the treasurer of the Court of Augmentations responsible for the vast church estates that had become Crown property, choosing a juicy plum for himself. Sir Edward North set about transforming the southern buildings into a palatial house by inserting a new court (27 × 23 metres), now Master's Court, where formerly there had been a small cloister. This is entered by the extant gateway under a range with a long gallery at first-floor level. Once in the court you are faced by the south-facing and handsome north range with its double-storeyed great hall and fine fenestration. At the first floor, north of the great hall, he created a generous room known as the great chamber over what had been the monastery frater. To the west he

did little to Wash-house Court and the surrounding service buildings. To the east of the new court he created another around the demolished Carthusian nave and choir, while maintaining the old tower and chapter-house, which was now turned into the chapel of the palatial residence. The whole created a rectangle, approximately a double square (c. 100 × 45 metres). Although many of these new rooms and ranges have been redecorated and altered in detail since the sixteenth century, they remain as the core of Sutton's Hospital.

Lord North died in 1564 and the Charterhouse was immediately purchased by Thomas Howard, Duke of Norfolk. Norfolk's main contribution to the architectural history of the site was the construction of what is now known as the Norfolk Cloister, northwards along the line of the west precinct passage. It is a barrel-vaulted brick structure with segmental arched openings and pedimented entrances to the central cloister garden. This melancholic range, with the remnants of blind doorways retained in the west wall that once opened into the monks' cells, terminated in a knot of spaces for leisure and pleasure. First there was a walled real tennis court, a game enthusiastically supported by Henry VIII with his own court at Hampton Court and by François I and his successor Henri II (reg. 1547–59) in France. There seems to have been a bathing house in cell G, and a banqueting suite. To complete this garden setting, there was a terrace walk on the roof of the cloistered walk: at 100 metres in length, it was longer than the equivalent galleries of other great Tudor houses and ended at the north end in a flight of steps into a wilderness garden. Elizabeth I succeeded to the throne in 1558 and it is known that she used the Charterhouse for five days as her headquarters before her triumphal entry into the City of London and then on to Westminster. Pondering her future, the terrace garden walk might well have played its part as a setting for her deliberations. The Norfolk Cloister is one of the most dramatic spaces of the Charterhouse but currently lacks a destination, terminating at half its original length

Fig 82: **Plan of the proposed cell garden, planted to create a destination at the far end of the Norfolk Cloister.**

Courtesy Eric Parry Architects

Fig 83: **The west wall of the Norfolk Cloister, the site of the proposed cell garden.**

Photograph by Tom Hobson

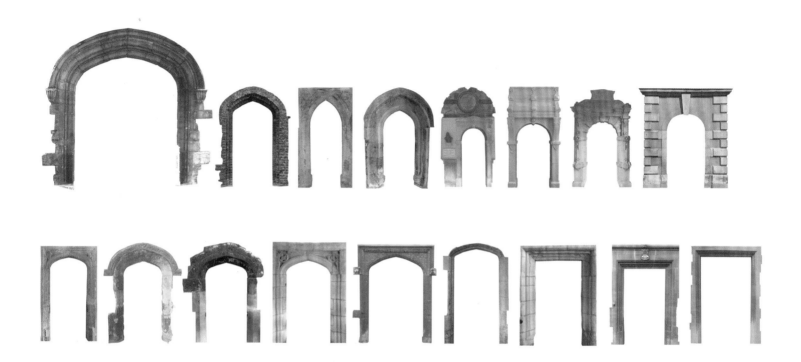

Top row (from left):

The Gatehouse; doorway by the Gatehouse; Cell B in the Norfolk Cloister; entrance to the Old Library; Chapel Cloister (north side); Old Library, entrance to the Norfolk Cloister; Chapel Cloister, (east side); Master's Court (north porch)

Bottom row (from left):

Staircase Hall (first floor); Master's Court (west side); entrance to Wash-house Court from the west; Staircase Hall (first floor); Master's Court (south side); entrance to Chapel Cloister; Staircase Hall (ground floor); Master's Court (north side); Chapel Court (east side).

Fig 84: **Charterhouse portals, a collage made in 2015 by the architects working on the 'Revealing' project.**

Courtesy Eric Parry Architects

at an uninviting Victorian brick wall. At the furthest reach of the 'Revealing the Charterhouse' project, a garden (Fig. 82) outlining the scale of one of the cells, together with the enclosing wall and a rill of water, is accessed through a doorway in the privy garden room at today's end of the cloister. To reinforce the historic length, a reflective glass wall is placed in front of the nineteenth-century brick wall, making the cloister appear twice its current length and therefore almost as it was in the fourteenth century. On the public tours, the moment of stepping through the wall between the cloister and the enclosure of a cell will be a powerful experience and emblematic of the project as a whole.

The west wall to the Norfolk Cloister (Fig. 83) is an extraordinary collage of the monastery cloister wall built in roughly coursed stonework, cell by cell as finances allowed. The evocative and finely carved pointed arched door surrounds and their serving hatches, together with floor hatches and surviving encaustic floor tiles, were definitively silenced by being bricked up. For 167 years these monks' cells doorways served their purpose of dividing two worlds: on one side the life of separation and contemplation, on the other the common cloister at the centre of which stood the conduit house from which, like the biblical four rivers of Eden, water flowed in conduits to the north, south, east and west, emerging in a concentrated and symbolic way in the gardens of the cells. This fresh water reawakened an energy for seeing, as light has greater clarity when it meets clear water.

DOORS AND THRESHOLDS

From the first introduction to the Charterhouse, reinforced by any number of subsequent visits, the rich palimpsest of the site in architectural terms, beyond the plan and arrangement of rooms, lies in the walls with their windows and particularly their doors. Where windows create light and views – sometimes monumental as in the case of the three-tiered Tudor oriel bay to the great hall, sometimes

diminutive as in the squint overlooking the high altar of the priory church from the first-floor Treasury – doors are the threshold between sometimes startlingly different settings. For the monastery the layers that form the outer walls, facing nature as at the Grande Chartreuse, or the city in the case of the London Charterhouse, ensure absolute solitude for the choir monks' cell garden, masking the extremes of public engagement and individual prayer. The Charterhouse gatehouse is a survivor of a form of urban threshold common to educational, monastic, military and palatial institutions. Most Oxbridge colleges still have their gatehouses, with a porter's lodge to one side, as is the case today at the Charterhouse's lodge, which is just big enough to house a seat and where outsiders are met to be escorted inwards through layered courts (courts in Cambridge, quads in Oxford, but either in London). The elevation to the square is typical of the juxtapositions and collaged historic layering of the whole site. The early fifteenth-century gateway, the stonework of which was revealed in the 1950s under the later stucco, has a segmental arch framing the ancient carriageway with a second of a similar scale masking the 'narrow way' beyond. To the right of the carriageway is the brick-framed pedestrian doorway that abuts the ancient chequerboard wall of Reigate stone and knapped flint. The physician's house, No 17 Charterhouse Square, built in the early eighteenth century and now the Master's Lodge, is a six-bayed frontage, three bays of which step back from the line of the gatehouse, the other three bays sitting atop the medieval gateway structure. The two parts of the latter are separated by a string course and flat hood that record the first transition from monastery to grand house. It makes a disturbing but wonderful collage of parts.

Set as the focus to chapel cloister, the very fine doorway between the cloister and antechapel was a part of the larger scheme drawn up by Francis Carter after the bequest of Thomas Sutton to transform the house into Sutton's Hospital in the Charterhouse; and specifically

Fig 85: Two elevations showing the north side of the
Square before and after the installation of the new
public entrance to the Charterhouse.

Courtesy Eric Parry Architects

at this point in the plan to expand the old monastery chapter-house northwards by the transformation of the wall into a screen of three arched openings. This was to accommodate the residents, young and old, and to house the very fine funerary monument to the benefactor. The antechapel, which is the lowest vaulted chamber of a series rising up the section of the tower to the belfry, is set within the wall thicknesses of the original tower. Originally the tower was given support on its south side by the priory church and then, once it became free standing, had successive additions to stabilise its mass. The doorway with its ornamented strapwork supports in a cartouche the monument to a former master by the mason Edmund Kinsman, working under Carter's general direction. All the craftsmen for the various trades of this seventeenth-century building campaign are recorded by name and their work crops up in several areas. Kinsman was also responsible, for example, for the fine chimneypiece in the great hall. The passage in the depth of the tower wall has hung on one side the remains of the charred timber door that is said to have saved the chapel beyond from the ravages of the fire in 1941.

PROPOSED NEW ENTRANCE

The new entrance for visitors (Fig. 85), clearly separated from the historic portered way to the west of the square, found its natural place on the unseen line described at the beginning of this essay as the point of equilibrium. This passes through the garden of Chapel Court to enter the buildings at the internal corner at the north-west of the court. This stone passage is a causeway raised a foot (0.3m) above the hallowed ground of the priory church; where the visitors reach a point in line with the axis of the reconstructed altar, they will find a stone ledger above the grave of Walter de Manny set in a bed of low cut hedging. A notice will alert those passing by to the significance of this vanished building, its purpose and its downfall:

You are looking towards the high altar. The granite slab marks the burial place of the priory's founder Sir Walter Manny, who died in 1372 … The Charterhouse was a centre of resistance to the King's religious reforms. The plaque on the far wall commemorates the 17 monks and lay brothers who chose to be put to death than to renounce their Catholic faith.

This terse summary marks the political surface of our history, with the Charterhouse one of the epicentres of the debate, that would shape in considerable part the modern world we find ourselves part of today. The significance of Chapel Court means it needs to be capable of being secured out of visiting hours. The nature of this openable, defensible line evolved through many iterations to the final choice of both the canopy (described below) and a rail, set at a height of 2.7 metres, on which the name of the Charterhouse could be placed flanked by bons mots from several of the benefactors and patrons, reflecting the changing views that have underpinned the life of this significant place.

When closed, the gates in the iron railings should still help the users of the square to understand what awaits them. On the northern boundary of the whole site, travelling along Clerkenwell Road, the small door in the massive brick wall with its memorable relief panels invites curiosity over the interiors, heightened when somebody slips in or out. Likewise, when standing at the railings to Chapel Court and the square there is no indication of the world that occupies the room between the two points. At an early stage it occurred to us that the idea of a cast model of the buildings and spaces between would be the best representation of the whole complex, particularly as much will remain inaccessible (Fig. 77). The model is placed as a tilted plane to be viewed from the square approach and clearly visible even when behind closed gates. The eye-catcher, the equivalent to the arched passageway of the historic gatehouse, was from the outset thought to be of a scale

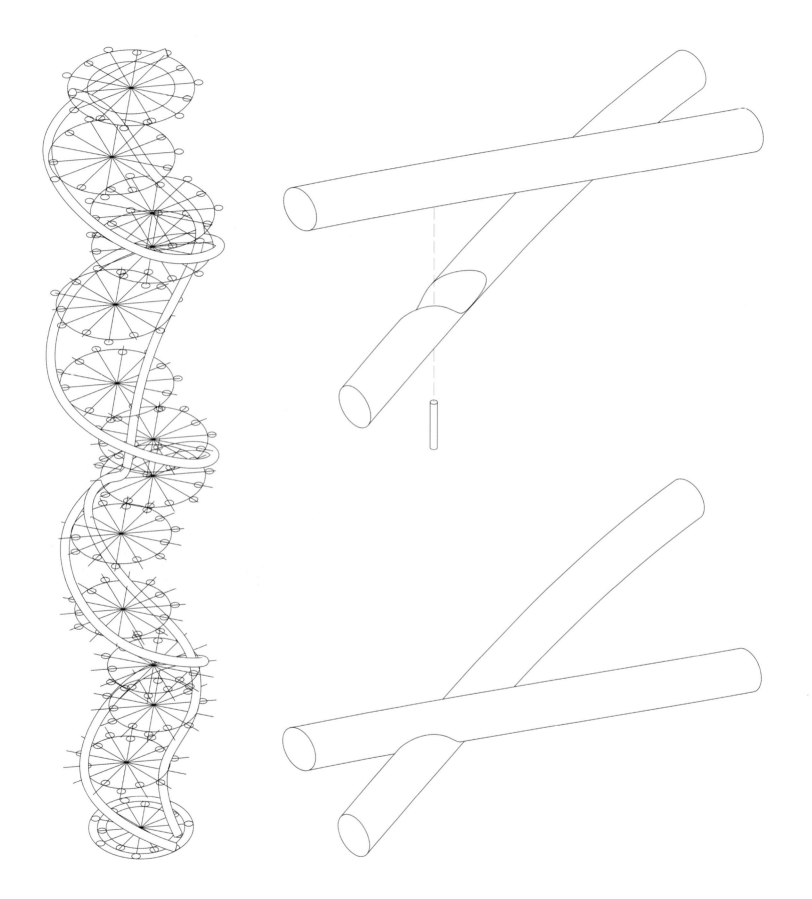

legible when viewed from across the square from the new path that acknowledges this new presence and entrance. It has developed as a room-sized canopy, unwittingly similar in scale to the vaulted chambers of the belfry tower. It has metamorphosed as the design progressed from a trabeated table with an oculus to the continuous bower of woven metal bars illustrated here (Fig. 87). As with a bower growing from stems at the four corners, the four supports, through the form of a segmented arch, rise to join in the layers of the canopy above. At the centre they descend slightly to support a large, white, vitreous enamel domed glass cover to a multiple-mantled gas lamp. The light here will be more intense than the other gas lamps in the square, in a manner equivalent to the two standards marking the present entrance. The metal bars are forged as they twist and weave; the finish is dark and lustrous. The spiral form is a reminder of the idea of continuity. In Christian iconography the appearance of a spiral column has long been a reference to the columns of Solomon's temple, marking the Holy of Holies containing the Ark of the Covenant. Columns of this type seem to have been installed in the basilica of Old St Peter's in Rome, partly demolished during the sixteenth century. Similar examples can be seen in illuminated manuscripts, Raphael's cartoon of *St Peter and St John Healing the Lame Man* (V&A), and most overtly in Bernini's baldacchino over what is commonly believed to be the titular saint's tomb in St Peter's, Rome. Reflecting these precedents at the Charterhouse, the canopy is a celebration of entry, standing over the fifteenth-century plan of the monastery, the outline of which is let into massive York stone slabs of the pavement to the same scale as the bronze model beyond.

Fig 86: **Details of the metalwork in the new canopy.**

Courtesy Eric Parry Architects

Fig 87: **3D printed model of the canopy marking the new public entrance to the Charterhouse.**

Courtesy Eric Parry Architects

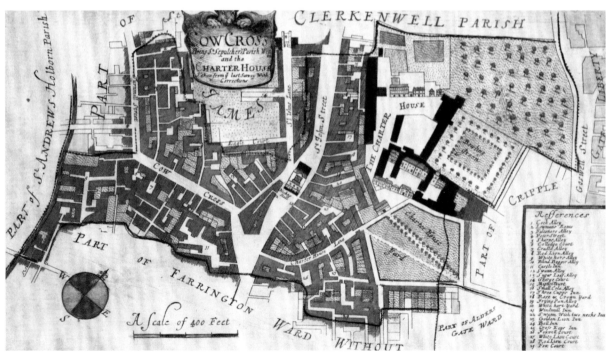

The Attraction of the 'ancient impenetrability' of Charterhouse Square

Todd Longstaffe-Gowan

Charterhouse Square is an unusual urban oasis. According to the historian Andrew Saint, writing in the *Survey of London* (2008), the open space, established in the fourteenth century, has kept its 'ancient impenetrability' with its unadopted roadways, its gates in three corners and its smattering of old houses. Through these it 'partakes of the air of a cathedral close, at one remove from urban bustle nearby'.[1] The square is, however, more than a mere forgotten corner in a great city – it is a place imbued with a remarkable atmosphere, redolent of great antiquity and pre-Reformation monasticism, and possessing an antiquarian interest unrivalled in other London squares. It is, moreover, exceptional in being the largest green space of a mosaic of yards, courts, gardens, walks and orchards, former kitchen gardens and wilderness, many of which were formed by the early seventeenth century, that make up the 3.5 hectare Charterhouse estate, which sits like a sprawling collegiate complex on the very edge of the City of London.

Like so many places of ancient habitation, the square has experienced its share of social and structural vicissitudes. Although it began to take its present shape in the third quarter of the seventeenth century, the irregular pentagonal garden has its origins in the Carthusian priory of the House of the Salutation of the Mother of God, formed in 1371, when it belonged to the priory's outer precinct. For several centuries it remained open ground, having served in the mid-fourteenth century as a burial place for victims of the Black Death. The freehold of the area, known variously before the 1720s as Charterhouse Churchyard, Charterhouse Precinct, Charterhouse Close or Charterhouse Yard, along with the Charterhouse itself, passed to Sir Edward North in 1538, soon after the dissolution of the monasteries, and then to the Duke of Norfolk in 1565. The priory therefore became a private mansion and its precincts a verdant forecourt to the same.

The so-called 'Agas Map' of London, made in the 1560s, indicates that by this time the area now occupied by Charterhouse Square was dotted with a few trees, possessed a chapel dedicated to the Virgin Mary and All Saints, and was enclosed on two sides by buildings and on the remaining sides by walls. In the wake of the dissolution the buildings surrounding the yard were inhabited by a handful of laymen and members of court circles: from about 1543 Henry VIII's sixth queen Katherine Parr and her brother William Parr are reputed to have lived in the yard, and so, too, did Sir John Williams, Keeper of the King's Jewels, Bartholomew Westby, Baron of the Exchequer, and John Leland, the noted topographer and 'King's Antiquary'.

From 1590 the yard was owned and managed by the Charterhouse governors, who in 1615–16 demolished the chapel and levelled the ground around it. Ten years later, in an effort to render the yard 'more neat and comely', a footpath flanked by wooden railings was cast across it to link the east gate to the square with the main gate of the Charterhouse.[2] Two sturdy gates controlled access to the precinct, one at Charterhouse Lane in the west and another at Carthusian Street in the east. From the mid-sixteenth century the former precinct was inhabited by residents of high status on account of its protected seclusion, its proximity to the Charterhouse and its immediate adjacency to the City. It retained this social pre-eminence for almost 150 years, being described in 1657 as containing 'many handsome Palaces, as *Rutland* House, and one where the *Venetian* Embassadors were used to lodge'.[3] The square's central area appears to have been improved by 1676, as it is depicted on Ogilby and Morgan's map of that year as enclosed by a post-and-rail fence, and bisected diagonally by an alley of trees.

Although in the late seventeenth century the square was on the whole well inhabited, its central yard, like so many similar open places across the metropolis (Lincoln's Inn Fields in particular), attracted a great deal of riff-raff; reports abound from the late sixteenth century to the late seventeenth of the residents being annoyed by 'the great resort

---

Fig 88: **The Square as laid out in the mid-eighteenth century, engraving by Sutton Nicholls, c.1750.**

Fig 89: **Plan of the Charterhouse and its Clerkenwell estate in 1755, including 'Charterhouse Yard'. Hand-coloured engraving.**

of evell disposed persons who doe play there daye and night', and who burgled their houses and made it unsafe to pass through the yard after dark. [4] The proximity to Smithfield Market, which Daniel Defoe informs us was, in 1726, 'without question, the greatest [livestock market] in the world', also brought about its share of problems: for instance in 1715 the residents were 'dayly annoyed with vast numbers of disorderly persons who teare down the Trees and fill it with noise and nastiness'. [5]

From 1687 the social and physical character of the square began to change with the demolition of a large mansion on the south-west side of the yard to create Hayne Street. This action and the redevelopment of four sides of the yard between 1688 and 1705 precipitated the flight of the enclave's aristocratic inhabitants and an influx of new residents of the middling sort. In 1715 thirteen of these proposed that the central area should be enclosed with a brick wall and palisades 'as in Leicester Square' in order to 'preserve the same in a decent manner'. [6] The measure appears to have had the desired effect, but by the early 1740s the central area was 'greatly neglected', and the palisade was so decayed that the residents were fearful that if it were 'permitted to be destroyed, the Square will become a Receptacle for Rubbish, Dirt, and Dunghills, and will be liable to be frequented by common Beggars, Vagabonds, and other disorderly Persons for the Exercise of their idle Diversions, and other unwarrantable Purposes, so as to be unfit for the Habitation of Persons of Character and Condition'. [7]

In an effort to improve the square, the inhabitants petitioned for and obtained an Act of Parliament to clean, pave, watch and to enclose the square in a 'more lasting and effectual manner'. [8] The 1742 Act proposed, among many things, that thirteen proprietors and inhabitants of premises around the square (including the Master, Register and Receiver of the Charterhouse) should be declared trustees with a view to putting the Act in execution. Under the new powers the central area was metamorphosed into a fashionable

London square: loose, idle or disorderly persons were evicted, and new rails were thrown up around the central area, which was spruced up and laid out with diagonal walks and planted with rows of trees. Access to the garden was henceforth strictly limited to key-holding residents, that is those who lived on the square and who contributed financially to its maintenance and improvement. The Act also forbade the tipping of rubbish, the grazing and exercising of livestock, and the 'use or exercise and Sport, Game or Diversion … to the Annoyance or Disturbance of the Inhabitants'. [9] Contemporary engravings record the results of the improvements, and mark the elevation of the former yard to the status of a square.

The square remained a fashionable quarter throughout the eighteenth century, and the historian Robert Smythe reports in the early nineteenth century that its inhabitants were 'of the most respectable description'. [10] However, from the 1840s the social character of the enclave once again began to change as family houses were given over to schools, lodging-houses and commercial premises. Things took a further turn for the worse with the cutting of the railway on the south side of the square in 1864–5 and the re-planning of Smithfield Market, which opened in 1868. These metropolitan improvements had a devastating impact on the character of what until then had been a sombre, dingy and silent backwater.

These assaults by the modern world may have in part contributed to the romanticisation of the precincts and its denizens, and galvanised contemporary writers and topographers to characterise the place as an oubliette into which to cast visions of the monkish past. George William MacArthur Reynolds revelled in the melancholic solemnity of the precincts. Writing in *The Mysteries of London* (1848), he reported that the 'vast cloistral buildings' in which 'eighty worn-out and decrepid persons who drag out the wretched remnant of their lives beneath the iron sway of a crushing ecclesiastical discipline', possessed a:

Fig 90: **The entrance to the Charterhouse showing the corner of the Square's gardens, from a view by William Westall engraved for Rudolph Ackermann's** *The History of the Colleges ... etc* (London, 1816).

mournful, gloomy and sombre appearance, which even the green foliage in the central enclosure cannot materially relieve. The houses are for the most part of antiquated structure and dingy hue – the windows and front-doors are small – and, pass by them when you will, you never behold a human countenance at any one of the casements. The curtains and the blinds, – and, in the winter time, glimpses of the fires burning in the parlours, – these are, to a certain extent, symptoms that the houses are tenanted: but no other farther signs of the fact can be discovered.[11]

Reynolds was not the only Victorian writer to be captivated by what Theodore Taylor described in 1864 as the 'old monkish character of the neighbourhood', and the gloomy appearance of the retired place.[12] *Knight's Cyclopædia of London* (1851) reports that Charterhouse Square is among the most spacious of the City's 'minikin open spaces with green turf on them, … which might delude a stranger with the notion that they were the first attempts at squares – something between the court and the square – child-squares'. The square, he remarked, had little life and humanity in its outward show, and the 'line of dead wall, the antique monastic building, the iron-gates at either entry into the square, and the soot-encumbered semi-vegetation of the trees, produce almost as depressing an effect as the sepulchral habitations of Bridgewater Square'.[13] A contributor to Charles Dickens's journal *Household Words* in 1852 was also struck by the square – 'a fortified position in the heart of London, made secure by an array of iron gates, and garrisoned by a well-victualled beadle'. It was 'nearly as quiet now, in the very core of the noisy City of London, as it was five hundred years ago, when it was a lonely field, bearing the name of "No Man's Land"'.[14]

The authors, like Knight and Thackeray, were fascinated by the monkish associations of the precinct, its 'scattered buildings, many old monastic walls', and its 'time-eaten cloisters, where monks spent an agony before death in the old grim days of persecution'.[15] Knight had a similar interest in the remote origins of the place, remarking that 'In the quiet of Charterhouse Square we are carried back to the time when knightly penitents sought consolation from its cloistered owners; when neighbouring Smithfield, instead of being a receptacle for live beef and mutton, was the scene of tournaments, and, yet more horribly attractive, of the triumph of those martyrs whose blood was the seed of the Reformed Church'.[16]

Many of the built features of the square that were so admired by the Victorians persisted until 1941, when parts of the Charterhouse were severely damaged during a heavy air raid on the City during the Second World War. The garden square itself remained reasonably unscathed, although it, too, sustained a direct hit by a high-explosive bomb in October 1940. Post-war redevelopment had in fact a much greater impact on the layout of the enclosure: most notably, the garden was decreased in size when the roadway round the square was widened to provide for roughly one hundred additional parking spaces. Encompassed by modern railings between 1949 and 1951, partially surrounded by regular blocks of holly hedging, and shaded by a range of semi-mature and mature trees, including a number of large mid-Victorian planes and a few sycamores, the central garden was until recently dull and uninteresting, and did little to complement the setting of the former priory. Indeed, the enclosure was so sterile that an ecological survey carried out in the late summer of 2014 determined that it comprised habitats that were 'generally considered to be of low ecological value'; and declared to be 'unsuitable for most protected species'. The avian ecology was only marginally more interesting: four species of bird were recorded – Carrion Crow, Feral Pigeon, Blue Tit and Blackbird – none of which is considered to be of conservation significance.[17]

In 2013 the Governors of the Charterhouse embarked on a campaign to open parts of the Charterhouse to the public, and to

Fig 91: **Postcard of the entrance gateway,** *c.*1920.

Fig 92: **Photograph of the entrance gateway,** *c.*1900.

improve dramatically the landscape of the square. I was fortunate to have been chosen to assist them in the latter regard.

The principal aims of our landscape refurbishment have been to improve significantly the quality of the Charterhouse precinct – and its landscape setting in particular – with a view to enhancing its secluded, precinctual air; to strengthen the visual and physical link between the square's central garden and the Charterhouse and other buildings that surround the square; to promote greater public access to the central private garden by opening it on a regular basis; to increase the area of the central garden by reducing the number of car parking spaces within the enclave; to make the gardens a more attractive and welcoming space to passers-by, residents of the square and potential visitors to the Charterhouse; and to encourage biodiversity through the introduction of semi-natural planting around the margins of the central garden, including planting a traditional country hedge alongside the perimeter railings.

The resultant scheme has been informed by an understanding of the historic development of the precinct, sensitivity to the character of the gardens, and adherence to current legislation regarding access, and health and safety. It is moreover a contemporary response to the Charterhouse and its surroundings, and the needs of a modern audience. The layout of these paths reflects the historic 'saltire' arrangement created in the early eighteenth century. The paths, which are laid to self-binding gravel and are a minimum width of 1.8 metres, provide improved access through the square, and are dotted with benches in the form of coiled serpents bearing the arms of the Carthusian order. The gates, two of which are new, have been placed with a view to providing easy access across the square and direct access from the south-west corner – the site of the Elizabeth Line station – to Chapel Court. Every effort has been made to provide reasonable access to the gardens, both physically and intellectually. Pedestrian access now

has priority throughout the precinct and the gardens and vehicular movement is being kept to a minimum. Provision has also been made for accessible parking bays and for drop-off facilities at Chapel Court.

The half-hectare central garden is open daily when the Charterhouse is open regularly to the public. This access gives considerable public benefit, as the gardens, which were until recently accessible only to rate-paying residents, lie within a London borough that is deficient in public open green space. The interior of the garden, very importantly, has been increased considerably by reclaiming space until recently occupied by more than one hundred car parking spaces.[18]

The gardens are managed by the Charterhouse's full-time gardener Claire Davies and her retinue of three to four volunteers and garden apprentices. A traditional 'square keeper' has been stationed in the enclosure at all times that the square is open to the public. The landscape scheme has been designed with a view to agreed staffing levels, and its simple and robust layout – although horticulturally rich – is intended to accommodate a significant increase in the gardens' day-to-day use. It has also been designed for environmentally sustainable maintenance and minimal irrigation. The garden maintenance plan will be reviewed independently and reported upon annually.

The garden square and the Charterhouse precincts are now almost entirely lit by gaslight. These lamps and standards, which have been placed at the entrance gates to the square and along the footpaths of the precinct, enhance immeasurably the special quality of the precinct. The lighting aims to reinforce the domestic quality of the square and to accentuate its distinctive character, marking its difference from the neighbouring streets.

Most of the area within the railings has been laid to grass, parts of which have been set aside and maintained as wildflower meadow. The aim throughout has been to maintain a rich and varied ecological structure to the gardens so as to increase their biodiversity value. The introduction

---

Fig 93: **An artist's impression of the Square after the 2016 replanting.**

Photograph courtesy Todd Longstaffe-Gowan

Fig 94: **Gardeners' tools.**

Photograph by Lawrence Watson

Fig 95: **Archaeologist excavating the site of a Black Death burial ground in Charterhouse Square, 2013.**

Photograph courtesy Crossrail Ltd.

of traditional English hedging – including hawthorn, blackthorn, holly, common privet, hazel, rowan and guelder rose – alongside the perimeter railings of the square, supplemented in stretches by densely planted broad shrubberies of native woodland species, including hawthorn, box, holly, crab-apple and elder, should enhance the biodiversity of the square by providing habitat for birds commonly associated with woodland or woodland-edge conditions. Naturalising bulbs, including *Narcissus poeticus*, *Camassia quamash* and *Scilla sibirica*, have been planted in the grass.

The central enclosure once again has a structure in its midst: an octagonal pavilion, soon to be smothered with living greenery, has been raised in its south-east corner.[19] The proposal to create a small eye-catcher was first mooted by Prince Charles, who, in his capacity as a Royal Governor of Sutton's Hospital in the Charterhouse, was keen to see something within the gardens that evoked the former presence of the fourteenth-century chapel. Our aim has been to create a garden cabinet, in the spirit of the late seventeenth century, which serves as both a shady retreat and a place in which to provide some interpretive material to provide insights into the history of the square. The pavilion, which was constructed by the blacksmiths Andrew Renwick and Paul Kardoosh and their team at Ridgeway Forge in Sheffield, is set immediately adjacent to the main and broadest gate into the garden, the primary entrance and exit point for visitors to the gardens and the precinct. A turned oak baluster surmounted by a four-sided pulpit sits at the centre of the pavilion. The former is inlaid with glazed ceramic tiles inscribed with brief histories of four of the most distinguished and influential residents of the square – namely Walter Manny (1300–1372), first Baron Manny, Edward North (1496–1564), first Baron North, Thomas Howard (1536–1572), fourth Duke of Norfolk, and Thomas Sutton (1532–1611) – whose shields of arms are emblazoned in *opus sectile*[20] laid in the pavilion floor. This heraldic tribute is flanked by panels of river cobbles, and the whole is encompassed by a stone band bearing the names of eight members of the Levett family, including Dr Henry Levett (1668–1725), one-time Chief Physician to the Charterhouse and generous benefactor to the same, and some of his recent and equally beneficent descendants (a handful of whom are former pupils of Charterhouse School).[21]

Whilst our various works have doubtless contributed to the improvement of the outward character of the square, what remains invisible within the landscape is equally compelling to the modern visitor. Crossrail's recent archaeological excavations have confirmed what has long been alleged, but never conclusively proven: that an as yet unknown number of bodies (possibly as many as 40,000) lie buried beneath the velvety lawns of the square. The remains are those of the victims of the Black Death, the 'raging great sweeping Pestilence, in the Reign of … *Edward* the third'.[22] This momentous discovery has piqued the public imagination and rekindled an interest in the early history of the Charterhouse, and the monastic period in particular: the excavation of the mortal remains of two dozen unfortunates, at least one of whom is believed to have been a monk, has breathed new life into the old place and reaffirmed the historical richness of the Charterhouse precincts.

The importance of the early origins of the square cannot be underestimated: they add a very special if intangible quality to the enclosure, an enduring quality that is reinforced by the enclave's insistent and sustained enclosure – what Saint has aptly described as an atmosphere of 'protected seclusion'. For centuries the enclave's gates and railings have served not only to protect it and its inhabitants, but also to create a symbolic boundary between the former monastery and the outer world. Charterhouse Square is a private estate into which the public are regularly invited, but it is at the same time an interstitial place situated between the public realm and the domestic gardens of the Brothers, with their own idiosyncratic interventions. To enter the gates of the square is to be transported to another world, a place of removal, a place that is conducive to meditativeness, and to thinking about and reimagining the remote past.

References

1   Philip Temple, *Survey of London*, XLVI: *South and East Clerkenwell* (London, 2008), 243.

2   James Howell, *Londinopolis: an historicall discourse or Perlustration of the City of London ...* (London, 1657), 343; London Metropolitan Archives, Corporation of London [LMA], Acc/1876/AR/1/5/1; for a detailed account of the area, see *Survey of London*, XLVI, 243-79.

3   Howell, *Londinopolis*, 343.

4   Kew, The National Archives, E164/45.

5   LMA, Acc/1876/G/3/4, f.6iv; Acc/1876/G/5/65/1.

6   Charterhouse Muniments, AOB, D, pp. 155-6: LMA, Acc/1876/G/5/65/1.

7   *Geo. II, Cap. VI*, An Act to enable the present and future Proprietors and Inhabitants of the Houses in Charterhouse Square, in the County of Middlesex, to make a Rate for raising Money effectually to inclose, pave, watch, clean and improve the said Square, and to continue the same in Repair.

8   Ibid.

9   Ibid.

10 Robert Smythe, *Historical Account of Charter-House: Compiled from the Works of Herne and Bearcroft, Harleian, Cottonian, and Private MSS. ...* (London, 1808), 290

11 George William MacArthur Reynolds, 'Two Unpleasant Lodgers', *The Mysteries of London*, IV (London, 1848), 151.

12 Theodore Taylor, *Thackeray: the Humourist and the Man of Letters* (London, 1864), 11.

13 Charles Knight, *Knight's Cyclopædia of London, 1851* (London, 1851), 749.

14 [William Thomas Moncrieff and Henry Morley], 'The Poor Brothers of the Charterhouse', *Household Words*, V, no. 116 (12 June 1852), 285.

15 Ibid., 286.

16 Knight, *Knight's Cyclopædia of London*, 749.

17 *The Charterhouse, London: Preliminary Ecological Assessment*, (Phase 1 Habitat and Protected Species Scoping Survey Report), prepared by MKA Ecology Limited, Shepreth, Hertfordshire (15 Sept. 2014), 2, 17.

18 760 square metres of land (formerly part of the central garden) has been taken back into the garden, increasing it from 4260 to 5020 square metres.

19 The structure has replaced a small and undistinguished twentieth-century wooden booth.

20 *Opus sectile* is the name given by the Romans to marble inlay in mosaic work that follows the lines of the pattern or picture, as opposed to the small fragments of stone or glass (tesserae) that fill in the rest of the design.

21 Christian C. Levett, Christian J. R. Levett, Charles Levett, Ashley Levett, Michael Levett, Rebecca Levett and Robert Levett.

22 Howell, *Londinopolis*, 342.

Figs 96, 97, 98: **Views of the gardens inside the Charterhouse.**

Photographs by Claire Davies

Following pages:

Fig 99: **The Head Gardener at work.**

Photograph by Lawrence Watson

a day in the life of the Charterhouse

4: evening

EVENING

6.30–7.30	Buffet supper set out for the Brothers in the great hall.
7.00–10.30	Various activities: Brothers' Reading Group (monthly); guests arrive for evening lectures, concerts or receptions in the great chamber.
10.30	The night porter locks the gates to Carthusian Street, checks the Square is empty, and that all guests have left. The entrance doors are locked.

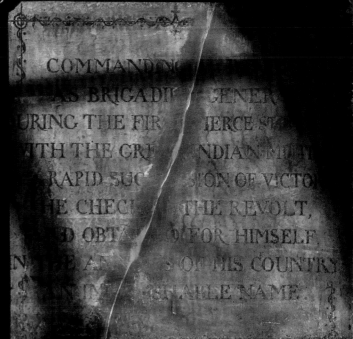

Fig 100: The Havelock Memorial in chapel cloister, erected in 1864 to commemorate former pupils of Charterhouse School who died in the Crimean War.

Photograph by Lawrence Watson

CONTRIBUTORS

Joe Ewart

Joe, the book's designer, studied painting at Chelsea School of Art and has worked as art director of *New Musical Express*, *Artscribe* and *Opera Now*. He designs for many arts organisations, including the National Gallery, National Portrait Gallery and the Victoria & Albert Museum. In 2012 he devised the new graphic branding for the Charterhouse and is retained as the institution's graphic designer; he works in a similar role for the Foundling Museum. Recent projects include the design of the monograph *Goya: the Portraits* (2015) for the National Gallery and the exhibition graphics for 'Revealing the Charterhouse'.

Nigel Llewellyn

Nigel Llewellyn BA MA MPhil PhD DLitt FSA undertook postgraduate training at Cambridge and at the Warburg Institute, where he was taught by E. H. Gombrich and Michael Baxandall. He taught art history for many years at the University of Sussex, where he also served as Dean of European Studies and as Pro-Vice-Chancellor. He recently retired from Tate where he established and ran the Research Department, 2007–15. He has published extensively on commemorative art and curated the *Art of Death* exhibition at the V&A in 1992. He now lives in Devon.

Todd Longstaffe-Gowan

Todd is a gardener and landscape historian. He is Gardens Adviser to Historic Royal Palaces with responsibilities at five royal palaces in Greater London, including Hampton Court and Kensington, Landscape Adviser to the Crown Estate Paving Commission in Regent's Park, and President of the London Parks and Gardens Trust. He is the author of several books, including *The London Town Garden, 1700–1840* (2001), *The Gardens and Parks at Hampton Court Palace* (2005) and *The London Square: Gardens in the Midst of Town* (2012).

Julian Luxford

Julian is Reader in Art History at the University of St Andrews. He has published widely on medieval subjects, but is particularly interested in the Carthusian order. Currently, he is writing a book on medieval drawings, and plans to follow this with a general, book-length study of the Carthusian order in the Middle Ages.

Eric Parry

Eric established Eric Parry Architects in 1983. Under his leadership, the practice has developed a reputation for delivering beautifully crafted and well-considered buildings that respond to their context. London has been the focus and the setting for most of his work. He was elected Royal Academician (RA) in 2006 and awarded the honorary degree of Doctor of Arts from the University of Bath in 2012. Eric also serves on the Kettle's Yard Committee, the Canterbury Cathedral Fabric Advisory Committee, the Mayor's Design Advisory Panel, the Council of the British School at Rome and is an Architecture Foundation Trustee.

Stephen Porter

Stephen has held research posts at the universities of Oxford and London. For seventeen years he was an Assistant Editor with the Survey of London and was then appointed Honorary Archivist at Sutton's Hospital. He has published a definitive history of the charity, *The London Charterhouse* (2009), along with several articles about Thomas Sutton and various aspects of his foundation. He is the author of numerous books on the history of London and the English Civil Wars, most recently *London: A History in Paintings & Illustrations* (2014) and *The Tower of London: The Biography* (2015). He is a Fellow of the Society of Antiquaries and of the Royal Historical Society. He is chairman of the Charterhouse's Heritage Committee.

Cathy Ross

Cathy is Honorary Research Fellow at the Museum of London, where she was Director of Collections and Learning until 2013. She was chief curator for the Museum of London's 'Galleries of Modern London', which opened in 2010, and has published widely on museums and London history. Books include *Twenties London: a City in the Jazz Age* (2003); *The Romance of Bethnal Green* (2007); *London: the Illustrated History* (2008); *Philanthropy: the City Story* (2013); and *Designing Utopia: John Hargrave and the Kibbo Kift* (2015). Cathy has been the curator for 'Revealing the Charterhouse'.

Catherine Smith

Catherine Smith has been the Archivist at Charterhouse School since 2009. Previously she has been the Archivist at Portsmouth Grammar School, Head of Advisory Service for the Business Archives Council and Assistant Registrar in the Royal Archives at Windsor. She studied History at the University of York and has a Master of Archives and Records Management from the University of Liverpool.

Lawrence Watson

Lawrence is a renowned photographer, best known for his contributions to the *New Musical Express* during its heyday in the 1980s. He has worked with such legendary bands and musicians as Paul Weller, Oasis, Pulp, Pet Shop Boys, Neneh Cherry, Grace Jones and George Clinton. An exhibition of his photographs documenting the life of Noel Gallagher over 18 months was shown in London in 2011, later touring to Tokyo. A selection of Lawrence's photographs since the 1980s were published under the title *The World is Yours* (2009).

Fig 101: Skull, carved above the gate to the old burial ground.

Photograph by Lawrence Watson

BIBLIOGRAPHY

Ackermann, Rudolph (publisher), *The History of the Colleges of Winchester, Eton, and Westminster; with the Charter-House, the Schools of St. Paul's, Merchant Taylors, Harrow, and Rugby, and the Free-School of Christ's Hospital* (London, 1816) [text by William Combe and others]

Archer, Ian W., *The Pursuit of Stability: Social Relations in Elizabethan London* (Cambridge, 1991)

—, 'The Arts and Acts of Memorialization in Early Modern London', in *Imagining Early Modern London: Perceptions and Portrayals of the City from Stow to Strype, 1598–1720*, ed. Julia Merritt (Cambridge, 2001)

—, 'The Charity of Early Modern Londoners', *Transactions of the Royal Historical Society*, 6th ser., XII (2002), 223–44

Arrowsmith, R. L., *A Charterhouse Miscellany* (London, 1982)

—, *Charterhouse Register, 1769–1872* (London and Chichester, 1974)

Aubrey, John, *Brief Lives*, ed. Richard Barber (London, 1975)

Bailey, Malcolm, *From Cloister to Cup Finals: a History of Charterhouse Football* (Shrewsbury, 2008)

Barber, Bruno, and Christopher Thomas, *The London Charterhouse*, Museum of London Archaeology Service Monograph 10 (London, 2002)

Barratt, Mark, and Chris Thomas, 'The London Charterhouse', *London Archaeologist*, VI/11 (1991), 283–91

Bearcroft, Philip, *An Historical Account of Thomas Sutton, Esq: and of his Foundation in Charter-House* (London, 1737)

Brown, Harold E. H. Haig, ed., *William Haig Brown of Charterhouse: A Short Biographical Memoir* (London, 1908)

Brown, W. Haig, *Charterhouse Past and Present* (Godalming, 1879)

—, *Carthusian Memories and Other Verses of Leisure* (London, 1905)

Burnet, Thomas, *A Relation of the Proceedings at Charter-House, upon Occasion of King James the II. His presenting a Papist to be admitted into that Hospital* (London, 1689)

Burrell, Percival, *Sutton's Synagogue, or, the English Centurion: shewing the un-parrallelled bounty of Protestant piety* (London, 1629)

'A Carthusian' [W.J.D.R.], *Chronicles of Charter-house* (London, 1847)

The Carthusian: A Miscellany in Prose and Verse, 2 vols (London, 1837–9)

Champneys, Basil, 'Old Charterhouse', *Magazine of Art*, XII (1886), 309–15

—, 'Charterhouse. Part I, The Monastery', 'Charterhouse. Part II, Spoliation: North, Howard and Sutton', *Architectural Review*, XI, nos 66–7 (1902), 171–81, 199–210

Chauncy, Maurice, *Historia aliquot nostri saeculi martyrum* (Mainz, 1550); Eng. trans. as *The History of the Sufferings of Eighteen Carthusians in England* (London and New York, 1890; repr., Whitefish, MT, 2010)

Coppack, Glyn, and Mick Aston, *Christ's Poor Men: the Carthusians in England* (Stroud, 2002)

Corke, Shirley, *Charterhouse-in-Southwark, 1884–2000: A Short History* (Godalming, 2001)

Davies, Gerald S., *Charterhouse in London: Monastery, Mansion, Hospital, School* (London, 1921)

Dillon, Anne, *Michelangelo and the English Martyrs* (Farnham, 2012)

Eardley-Wilmot, E. P., and E. C. Streatfield, *Charterhouse Old and New* (London, 1895)

Evans, Robert C., 'Thomas Sutton: Ben Jonson's Volpone?', *Philological Quarterly*, LXVIII (1989), 295–314

Fletcher, Hanslip, *Bombed London* (London, 1947)

Gibson, E.C.S., 'Thackeray and Charterhouse, with sidelights on the life of a public school a hundred years ago', *Cornhill Magazine*, 3rd ser., LII (June 1922), 641–59

Girdlestone, F.K.W., E. T. Hardman and A. H. Tod, eds, *Charterhouse Register, 1872–1900* (Godalming, 1904; rev., 1872–1910, 2 vols, 1911; rev., 1872–1931, 3 vols, 1932)

Grainger, Ian, and Christopher Phillpotts, *The Cistercian Abbey of St Mary Graces, East Smithfield, London*, Museum of London Archaeology Monograph 44 (London, 2011)

The Greyfriar (1884–) [Charterhouse School literary magazine]; 1884–1936 available at http://charterhouse.daisy.websds.net

Hale, William Hale, 'The Carthusian Monastery of London', *Transactions of the London and Middlesex Archaeological Society*, III (1869), 309–31

[—], *Some Account of the Early History and Foundation of the Hospital of King James, Founded in Charterhouse* (London, 1854)

Hendriks, L, *The London Charterhouse, its Monks and its Martyrs* (London, 1889)

Herne, Samuel, *Domus Carthusiana, or, an account of the Most Noble Foundation of the Charter-House ... with the life ... of Thomas Sutton, esq., the founder thereof ...* (London, 1677)

Hope, William St John, *The History of the London Charterhouse from its Foundation until the Suppression of the Monastery* (London, 1925)

—, 'The London Charterhouse and its Old Water Supply', *Archaeologia*, LVIII/1 (1902), 293-312

Hotine, Margaret, 'Ben Jonson, Volpone, and Charterhouse', *Notes & Queries*, n. s., XXXVIII/1 (1991), 79-81

Howell, James, *Londinopolis: an historicall discourse or Perlustration of the City of London ...* (London, 1657)

Knight, Charles, *Knight's Cyclopædia of London, 1851* (London, 1851)

Knowles, David, 'The London Charterhouse', in *The Victoria History of the County of Middlesex*, I, ed. J. S. Cockburn et al. (London, 1969), 159-69.

Knowles, David, and W. F. Grimes, *Charterhouse: The Medieval Foundation in the Light of Recent Discoveries* (London, 1954)

Lasocki, David, with Roger Prior, *The Bassanos: Venetian Musicians and Instrument Makers in England, 1531-1665* (Aldershot, 1995)

Llewellyn, Nigel, *Funeral Monuments in Post Reformation England* (Cambridge, 2000)

Longstaffe-Gowan, Todd, *The London Square: Gardens in the Midst of Town* (New Haven, CT, 2012)

Luxford, Julian M., ed., *Studies in Carthusian Monasticism during the Late Middle Ages*, Medieval Church Studies 14 (Turnhout, 2008)

—, 'The Space of the Tomb in Carthusian Consciousness', in *Ritual and Space: Proceedings of the 2009 Harlaxton Symposium*, ed. F. Andrews (Donington, 2011), 259-81

March, Bower, and Frederick Arthur Crisp, eds, *Alumni Carthusiani: A Record of the Foundation Scholars of Charterhouse, 1614-1872* ([London], 1913)

[Moncrieff, William Thomas, and Henry Morley], 'The Poor Brothers of the Charterhouse', *Household Words*, V, no. 116 (12 June 1852), 285-91

Oswald, Arthur, 'The London Charterhouse Restored', *Country Life*, CXXVI (1 Oct. 1959), 418-21; (8 Oct. 1959), 478-81; repr., London, 1959

Papers from Greyfriars (1860-61) [Charterhouse School literary magazine]

Patrick, George, 'The History and Architecture of the Charter-House', *Journal of the British Archaeological Association*, n. s., III (1897), 281-90

Porter, Stephen, *The London Charterhouse* (Stroud, 2009)

—, 'Order and Disorder in the Early Modern Almshouse: The Charterhouse Example', *London Journal*, XXIII/1 (1998), 1-14

—, 'Composer in Residence: Henry Purcell and the Charterhouse', *Musical Times*, CXXXIX, no. 1865 (1998), 14-17

—, 'Planning for a Monument: Dr John King and Charterhouse Chapel', *Transactions of the Ancient Monuments Society*, XLVII (2003), 33-46

—, 'Francis Beaumont's Monument in Charterhouse Chapel and Elizabeth, Baroness Cramond as Patroness of Memorials in Early Stuart London', *Transactions of the London and Middlesex Archaeological Society*, LIV (2003), 111-19

—, and Adam White, 'John Colt and the Charterhouse Chapel', *Architectural History*, 44 (2001), 228-36

Quick, Anthony, *Charterhouse: A History of the School* (London, 1990)

Radclyffe, Charles W., *Memorials of Charterhouse: a series of original views taken and drawn on stone* (London, 1844)

Reynolds, George William MacArthur, 'Two Unpleasant Lodgers', 'The Captain's Ludicrous Adventure', 'The Charter House', *The Mysteries of London*, IV (London, 1848), 151-68

Seely, Henry J. A., Baron Mottistone, 'The ancient buildings of the London Charterhouse', *Journal of the London Society*, no.311 (December 1951), 97-107

Shipley, Neal R., '"Full Hand and Worthy Purposes": the Foundation of Charterhouse, 1610-1616', *Guildhall Studies in London History*, I/4 (1975), 229-49

—, 'Thomas Sutton: Tudor-Stuart Moneylender', *Business History Review*, I/4 (1976), 456-76

—, 'The History of a Manor: Castle Campes, 1580-1629', *Bulletin of the Institute of Historical Research*, XLVIII (1975), 162-81

—, 'A Possible Source for *Volpone*', *Notes & Queries*, XXXIX/3 (1992), 363-9

Smythe, Robert, *Historical Account of Charter-House: Compiled from the Works of Herne and Bearcroft, Harleian, Cottonian, and Private MSS. ...* (London, 1808)

Stow, John, *A Survey of London* (London, 1603); ed. C. L. Kingsford (Oxford, 1908)

Taylor, D. J., *Thackeray* (London, 1999)

Taylor, William F., *The Charterhouse of London: Monastery, Palace and Thomas Sutton's Foundation* (London, 1912)

Temple, Philip, *The Charterhouse*, Survey of London Monograph 18 (New Haven, CT, 2010)

—, *Survey of London*, XLVI: *South and East Clerkenwell* (London, 2008)

Thackeray, William Makepeace, *The Newcomes* (London, 1855)

Thompson, E. Margaret, *The Carthusian Order in England* (London, 1930)

Thornbury, Walter, and Edward Walford, *Old and New London*, 6 vols (London, 1897)

Tod, A. H., *Charterhouse* (London, 1900)

Trevor-Roper, H. R., 'Thomas Sutton', *The Carthusian* (Oct. 1948), 2–8

—, 'The Bishopric of Durham and the Capitalist Reformation', *Durham University Journal*, XXXVIII (1946), 45–58; rev. *Durham Research Review*, V/18 (1967), 103–16

—, 'Sutton, Thomas (1532–1611)', *Oxford Dictionary of National Biography* (Oxford, 2004)

Adam White, 'A Biographical Dictionary of London Tomb Sculptors, c.1560–c.1600', *Walpole Society*, LXI (1999), 1–161

Williams, Neville, *Thomas Howard, Fourth Duke of Norfolk* (London and New York, 1964); repr. as *A Tudor Tragedy: Thomas Howard, Fourth Duke of Norfolk* (London, 1989)

Wines, Andrew, 'The London Charterhouse in the Later Middle Ages: an Institutional History', PhD thesis, U. Cambridge, 1998

—, 'The Founders of the London Charterhouse', in *Studies in Carthusian Monasticism in the Late Middle Ages*, ed. J. Luxford, Medieval Church Studies 14 (Turnhout, 2008), 61–71

Zillekens, Ernst, ed., *Charterhouse: A 400th Anniversary Portrait* (London, 2010)

GOVERNORS OF THE CHARTERHOUSE, APRIL 2016

Royal Governors

Her Majesty the Queen
His Royal Highness The Duke of Edinburgh
His Royal Highness The Prince of Wales

Archiepiscopal Governors

The Archbishop of Canterbury, The Most Reverend and Right Honourable
Justin Welby MA

Patrons

The Duke of Norfolk
Michael Cassidy CBE
The Right Reverend and Right Honourable Richard Chartres KCVO DD FSA
George Von Mallinckrodt KBE KCSG

Governors

Air Chief Marshal Sir Michael Graydon GCB CBE FRAeS *Chairman*
The Right Honourable The Lord Wakeham PC JP DL FCA
Paul Double LLM
Sir John Banham DL
The Marquess of Salisbury KCVO PC DL
Dr Clare Heath MA MBBS MRCGP
The Lord Glenarthur DL
Timothy Boxell LLB
Daniel Hodson MA FCT
Simon Kitching FRICS
Michael Power ACA
Peter Hodgson CBE FCA DL
Caroline Cassels LVO GN DMS
Baroness Andrews OBE

Development Board

Wilf Weeks OBE *Chairman*
Baroness Andrews OBE
Mark Hix
Beatrice Hollond MA (Oxon)
Dr Jonathan Hunt MA BM BCh
Joyce Hytner OBE
Alderman Neil Redcliffe
Alderman William Russell
Allen Sanginés-Krause
Richard Wilkin LVO MBE DL

CHR·HOUSE

Fig 102: A carpenter's plane, stamped with the Charterhouse's mark.

Photograph by Lawrence Watson

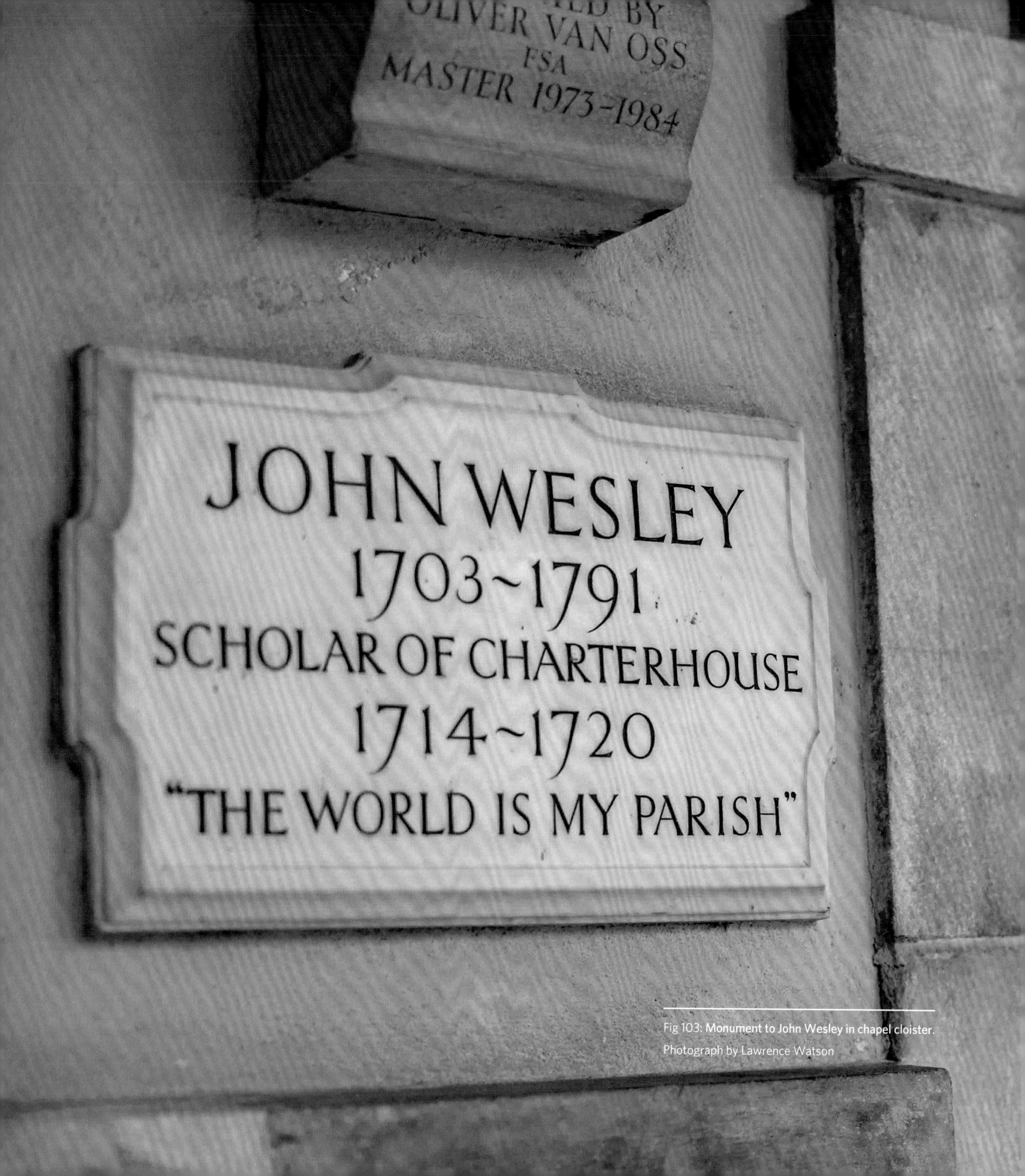

OLIVER VAN OSS
FSA
MASTER 1973~1984

JOHN WESLEY
1703~1791
SCHOLAR OF CHARTERHOUSE
1714~1720
"THE WORLD IS MY PARISH"

Fig 103: Monument to John Wesley in chapel cloister.
Photograph by Lawrence Watson

INDEX